Contents

Preface

Since the publication in 1989 of *Bullying in School* (edited by Tattum and Lane) there has been much research and many words written about bullying behaviour in schools. There have been great strides made in the understanding of the nature of bullying, the effects the behaviour has on children and the strategies that can be adopted to tackle the problem in schools. Much of this work has concentrated on the 15 per cent of the school population said to be involved in the behaviour.

The effect of this work has been significant. All schools are now requested to explain to parents and others how they tackle the problem of bullying behaviour. It is now rarely seen as an admission of failure if a school informs parents of what it is doing to minimise the effects of bullying. One element in an OFSTED inspector's brief is to examine the nature and effectiveness of the school's stated anti-bullying policy – evidence, if more were needed – of the determination amongst decision makers to minimise the effects of anti-social behaviour.

It is not only in the nation's schools that tackling the problem of bullying has risen to prominence. The prevalence and effects of bullying behaviour have also been investigated in the home, in the work place, in the armed forces, and in prisons. Some chapters in this book are testimony to the nature and effects of these new lines of work.

By titling the present book *Bullying: Home, School and Community* the editors wished to draw attention to the fact that the behaviour of an individual cannot be taken out of the social context in which that behaviour takes place. Bullying behaviour, whether perpetrated by an individual or groups of individuals, cannot be divorced from the behaviours which occur in the home, other behaviours in school and behaviours which take place in the community generally. Inevitably, there is an overlap and to some extent 'Home, School and Community' is an artificial construct. Nevertheless, the title highlights the complex nature of examining the deviant behaviour we call bullying.

The contributors to the book have worked for many years at tackling the results of bullying behaviour or at trying to minimise the effects. Some of the chapters are the result of detailed and analytical research. Other chapters highlight the daily problems of working with groups of children and adults who may have different views about the importance of tackling the behaviour. Despite the lack of rigorous research techniques in these areas, the work nevertheless shows a trend which reflects the findings of more detailed research.

Chapter 1 examines bullying behaviour from the premise that it is an endemic community problem which is imported into schools and, particularly in secondary schools, is resistant to change. It analyses parenting styles, highlighting those which promote bullying behaviour, as well as providing intervention strategies which will help very young children. It also presents relationships which will promote pro-social behaviour.

An account of the problems associated with home–school liaison, is the subject matter of Chapter 2. The work of a home–school liaison teacher shows how there was an improvement in parenting styles and the positive effects this had on children's behaviour. It then proceeds to provide ways of analysing the success of such interventions.

In Chapter 3, workers from a family service unit recount how they tackled bullying through play groups, enlisting the help of the parents, others in the community and local schools.

Chapter 4 concludes Part 1 and prepares us for the section on the school by dealing with transfer from home to school and how each institution can prepare the child for this experience.

A psychological perspective of tackling bullying behaviour and its consequences in school is adopted in Chapter 5. It highlights the impact of language in bullying situations as well as giving strategies which can be employed to condemn the behaviour. Finally, approaches to help support the victim of verbal bullying are considered.

Chapter 6 describes a multi-disciplinary approach to preventive work with primary school children. It gives a number of strategies which support social skills training amongst vulnerable children.

A holistic approach which supports the curriculum through the development of social skills and core skills is presented in Chapter 7. The strategies outlined offer power and responsibility to pupils and individuals rather than to adults and professionals. One case study shows the positive effects the approach had across an entire community.

An examination of the concepts of counselling and peer counselling lies at the heart of Chapter 8. The need for an holistic, integrated approach is presented. It is concluded by stating that there can be no simplistic solutions to bullying since the behaviour cannot be divorced from its social context.

The summary of a longitudinal study covering 14 different schools is encompassed by Chapter 9. The co-ordinator of a 'Safer City' Project gives his account of introducing anti-bullying programmes in a number of schools. The effect these strategies had on pupil behaviour is also recounted, together with the effective processes of introducing whole-school strategies. This chapter concludes Part 2.

Chapter 10 recounts the work of a family service unit which stemmed from the complaints of some vulnerable children. Although the work was deemed successful, the workers realised the need to develop a community-wide approach to tackling bullying, thereby ensuring a consistency of approach.

A different perspective is given in Chapter 11. Here, the effects on pupil behaviour are outlined by police–school liaison officers and their attempts at introducing a 'School Watch'. The work stresses the importance of children's perceptions at the same time as stressing the positive effect upon behaviour which such initiatives can have.

The work of the Heartstone Trust is presented in Chapter 12. The positive effects of the 'Heartstone Odyssey' on the behaviour of children in schools, youth clubs and children's homes is recounted.

The long-term effects of bullying behaviour are examined in Chapter 13. There is an analysis of the relationship between bullying behaviour, particularly in secondary schools, and subsequent criminality. There is a detailed analysis of a survey of 250 inmates. Among the topics discussed are bullying by teachers, family relationships, parenting styles, children with special educational needs and the pernicious effects of peer pressure.

The final chapter analyses the effects of interventions at a Young Offenders' Institute at Cardiff Prison. The dramatic reductions in suicide attempts and acts of self-harm and self-mutilation are evidence of the effectiveness of an anti-bullying programme. A number of strategies, both reactive and proactive, are presented, along with their aims and successes.

The scope of the book is therefore wide. It ranges from detailed case studies which highlight a particular trend to thorough and rigorous research. All chapters, however, underline the editors' views that the complex nature of bullying behaviour cannot be divorced from the social interactions, the relationships and the patterns of behaviour of a whole community. To attempt to isolate an individual act or bully the bully are simplistic in conception and will probably exacerbate the problem rather than improve it.

Graham Herbert, October 1996

List of contributors

George Ball, Reader in Education, University of Wales Institute, Cardiff

Shirley Barry, Inspector, South Wales Police.

Michael Bolton, Lecturer, Psychology Department, Keele University.

Daniel Cremin, Community Development Consultant, Birmingham

Angela Devlin, Criminology Researcher, Waterside Press, Winchester.

Kay Fitzherbert, Director, National Pyramid Trust.

Jim Fletcher, Constable, South Wales Police

Gerry German, Former Principal Education Officer, Commission for Racial Equality.

David Hawker, Post-graduate Researcher, Psychology Department, Keele University.

Graham Herbert, Senior Teacher, Saladine Nook High School, Huddersfield.

Sita Kumari, Director of the Heartstone Project. Alwyn Morgan, School Community Officer, Hull.

Charlie Naish, Constable, South Wales Police

Jackie Piccos, Special Needs Co-ordinator, Stockwell Primary School, Hull.

Pete Randall, Director. Family Assessment and Support Unit. University of Hull.

Martin Richards, Social Worker. Wakefield Social Services.

Pat Robinson, Co-director, Catalyst Training and Consultancy, Birmingham.

Maggie Robinson, Lecturer, School of Education, University of Durham.

Graham Smith, Educational Psychologist. Wolverhampton

Hilary Stacey, Co-director, Catalyst Training and Consultancy, Birmingham.

Delwyn Tattum, Co-director, Countering Bullying Unit, U.W.I.C.

Eva Tattum, Co-director, Countering Bullying Unit, U.W.I.C.

Louise Warner, Group Worker, West Leeds Family Service Unit.

Ted Walsh, Community Worker, Thurrock Family Service Unit.

Sue Yeo, Project Manager, National Pyramid Trust.

PART I

HOME

Introduction by Delwyn Tattum

This introduction on the home, prefaces four chapters predominantly on the early years, but it is not intended that this introduction should be exclusively about pre-school aged children but about what influences the home has upon children who become bullies or victims during their subsequent years of schooling. And, in that way, the introductions to the three sections of the book may be read in combination, as they aim to offer an integrated theme from preparing for school until adolescence. They are not intended as summaries of the chapters, these will speak for themselves, but as a means of introducing some new thoughts on the problems relevant to the theme of the section.

The last chapter in this book describes an anti-bullying programme in a Young Offenders' Institution (YOI) and Figure 14.3, the model of the Cycle of Violence, illustrates the cyclic career of many young bullies who continue through the ages into adolescent offenders and on to a life of violent adult crime. Many of these young men become fathers and, as Farrington (1991) demonstrates, continue in significant numbers to abuse their families and start the cycle again through teaching by example that aggression is a 'normal' way of behaving! How much better if we concentrated more of our efforts on preventative programmes by intervening in the early years. That is, by providing pre-nursery education and even parenting courses for young adolescents and new parents. Our national aim should be to finance more early years programmes rather than building more boot camps. For money spent on nursery education works better than prison, since it is preventative. The American Head Start programme, started over 30 years ago, targeted children in the most run-down, crime-prone communities and provided them with two years intensive nursery education. In a longitudinal study, the children were followed through to adulthood, and many have done well in their personal lives. They have committed 30 per cent less crime, they are five times less likely to draw welfare, they own their own homes and keep down good jobs. That in itself is a significant outcome in human, let alone, national terms.

Bullies are not born, they are created by those most influential in their lives – and the persons providing the most influential role models in a child's formative years are parents or carers. Children may be born with psychoneurological conditions, such as, hyperactivity, attention deficit disorder and so on, but it is the nature of the home climate created by the adults (parents) that has the major bearing on the development of a bully. It is believed that attitudes and values regarding aggressive behaviour are hardened and entrenched by junior school age and therefore secondary school may be too late. Therefore prevention is again the best approach, that is provision of appropriate early education to negate aggressive tendencies, especially for children who are regarded as 'at risk' because of the socio-economic circumstances of the family; and parenting courses for teenagers and for parents in the community before bad behaviour is learned and acted out.

The majority of bullies come from homes that are abusive and violent, where parents are authoritarian, inconsistent, negative or indifferent. Discipline is harsh and inconsistent – there is too little love and too much rejection. The limits of acceptable behaviour vary with mood and the children are confused by the warm–cold response of authority figures. Discipline is physically aggressive and parents often argue and abuse each other. In recent studies of battered wives, fathers have drawn the children into the physical and verbal bullying of their mothers.

In such homes where a physical response is accepted, the adults have little understanding of the harmful effects of physical punishment. They think spanking is fine, when really they only demonstrate that the person with the bigger stick gets his or her own way. Excessive use of spanking also injects hostility and resentment into a relationship, which is then re-enacted on the school playground. In fact, the links between school bullies and adult bullies is developed in Chapter 1. Children can become locked into a bullying family tradition. It can be the case, as many schools have found to their cost, that many bullying parents see their son's or daughter's behaviour as admirable – 'A chip off the old block'. Their response is often that they taught their child to get in the first insult or blow. This is a very difficult dilemma because it can result in the school punishing a pupil for behaving in a way the parents wholeheartedly support, which makes resolution of a difficult problem even more complex.

In many ways it is a defensive action where the neighbourhood requires its citizens to be rough and tough in order to survive in a physically and socially hostile atmosphere. Some of the studies in this section describe such neighbourhoods that are not safe, and survival demands a protective shell of aggressiveness. Similarly, with the increase in single mothers and a decline in the immediacy of an extended family a young boy may be missing an appropriate male role in the home. They may be left unsupervised for long periods, while mother is out working, and become bored and uncontrolled. Older siblings frequently bully young children, once again demonstrating that the only way to gain control is through being prepared to wield a big stick.

Aggressive children display their aggression in many ways. Children who are bullies will wreak their abuse on teachers and so disrupt the class. Similarly, bullies have scant regard for other people's property which results in petty theft and vandalism. Thus the persistent bully may also be a disrupter, thief and vandal – that is, a threat to the good order of a school. Equally, children who are bullied may refuse to attend school or, when they get older, may become persistent truants. In these ways, the behaviour of a bully can have long-term adverse effects on a range of people; and how long those harmful memories can have an inter-generational effect can be seen in the results in a recent pilot survey of parents conducted by the National Confederation of Parent Teacher Associations (1996). They received 1,186 returns which accounts for 10 per cent of their circulation to 11,000 member schools. Unsurprisingly, the majority (80 per cent) of the returns came from women who spoke of a cycle of misery. Some 62 per cent described how they had been bullied in school and almost 60 per cent of their children had also been bullied. Those parents who had been bullied and responded to the survey were more than twice as likely to have children who have been bullied. One wonders to what extent they transmitted their personal anxieties to their children. And as the report acknowledges, we must be wary of applying these figures on a national basis, as it is possible that it was a self-selecting sample of respondents.

The above data reflects the way in which bullying can remain with an individual into adulthood and the memory continue to be a blight on their family lives. For 23 per cent of parents the effects on them were long-term and for some these were never resolved. They experienced unresolved anger and resentment, and there was a great loss of confidence and often an inability to make friends as they felt that people could not possibly like them. For bullying not only affects the victim but the whole family often suffers the hurt.

> A bullied child tends to disrupt life, causing stress at home due to mood swings, aggressive behaviour and refusal to help in the home. Often children are tearful, sometimes crying frequently or irritable and bad tempered. They pick on younger siblings, lashing out in an attempt to vent their frustrations. In extreme cases toys and possessions around the home are hidden or go missing, or extra money is requested. (NCPTA, 1996)

And we may add that in extreme cases children may try to commit suicide, and in some instances succeed in taking their own lives.

Finally, a survey into health and bullying was conducted by the School Health Education Unit at Exeter University. The survey (Balding *et al.*, 1996) involved 11,613 pupils in a range of secondary schools in seven local authorities distributed throughout England. The 65 schools that participated covered ages 11 to 16 years, and represented ability groups, social class and ethnicity. On health matters they found clear links to higher frequency of illness and disease, and referral to the doctor was evident among those most likely to fear bullying. And in favour of a model of the family where children experience shared support for their well-being from both their mother and father, the report linked traditional family life as a source of confidence building, low levels of anxiety and fear of being bullied at school.

CHAPTER 1

Pre-school children: experiences of being parented and the routes to bullying

Pete Randall

Despite the popular mythology created by the media and those who seek to portray schools as the breeding grounds of bullies, there is considerable evidence that the roots of much bullying are nurtured in the homes of perpetrators where aggression is learned and honed by deviousness into bullying. In some areas, characterised by high levels of aggression, bullying is an endemic community problem imported into schools and fiercely resistant to change (Randall, 1996). The purpose of this chapter is to examine the roots of the early aggression that becomes bullying by demonstrating the variety of parenting experiences associated with it. The 'Theory of Mind' model of cognitive dysfunction is used to typify one major result of these experiences and suggests an approach for promoting better social learning.

The development of aggression and its inhibitors

Human aggression does not manifest itself as a fully-formed schema of activity; instead it is the product of observable developmental phases, each of which develops alongside mediators of aggression that normally keeps it in check (Landy and Peters, 1992).

If a combination of biological and environmental factors are optimal then children's aggression becomes channelled into assertiveness or only arises appropriately in response to severe provocations or threats. The role of the primary carers is to ensure that this optimal combination is realised. The quality of their own behaviours and interactions with the child are of paramount importance. This remains true from the earliest interactions during infancy onwards through adolescence. Although there is no single successful pattern of interactions, certain principles are important. These include:

- The earliest contacts of the infant with the primary care-giver, usually the mother, are vital because they provide a high level of response to the infant's needs at a physical level. If these contacts are satisfactory the patterns of interaction begin to be formed that later develop into social relationships and styles of interacting with other people (Tronick, 1989).

- Tronick also makes the point that a happy emotional tone conveyed through loving affection during these early contacts between infants and care-givers is crucial for the formation of attachment, the regulation of behaviour and emotional development in general. Parents who are happy to be with their infants and use soothing interactions when they are distressed are more likely to transform unhappy, negative emotional states into more positive ones, particularly when frustration, sadness and anger are liable to overwhelm the infant.

- Infants are helped to tolerate negative and frustrating occurrences because of the support they gain from high quality interactions from primary care-givers. Later on language becomes important in these interactions, such that the infants are able to use language or pretend play in a manner which reduces frustration. Gradually the nature of the interactions, if successful, shows them that they have a right to express anger but encourages more symbolic ways of doing this than through displays of overt aggression. Language enables children to 'label' their feelings and so reduces the need to express them physically in terms of aggression.

- The quality of interaction also should enable children to develop independence whilst at the same time acknowledging their need for security. In teaching children that they may explore in safety, a message is conveyed that there is no need to resort to aggression or other strong emotions in order to regain the security of contact with the primary care-givers.

- It is also the case that the behaviour of primary care-givers is a potent model for the children's own behaviour. Thus adults who model empathy, turn-taking, comforting, negotiation and caring promote pro-social behaviours that are incompatible with the physical expression of anger through aggression. Ultimately such learning will help children to terminate their aggression in order to avoid causing other people pain or distress.

- The quality of interaction between care-givers and children is also established through the way in which limitations on the children are set and maintained. High quality interactions provide children with the security of known limits and the assurance of reinforcement for correctly identifying those limits and behaving within them. Consistent sanctions discourage acts of aggression and consistent reinforcement encourages pro-social behaviour. Although some care-givers may not be aware of the learning theories on which this social teaching is constructed, they are nevertheless able to devise appropriate strategies for maintaining the consistency that is needed.

Adverse parenting styles

It is clear that primary care-givers, usually parents, have a considerable role and responsibility for the development of children's ability to inhibit aggression. Their style of interaction with children will help them become individuals able to take a normal and co-operative place in their community. The fact that there is an increasing number of pre-school children entering educational provision with significant aggressive conduct disorders (McQuire and Richman, 1986) indicates that this process is all too frequently going wrong. One of the reasons for this seems to be bound up in the kinds of beliefs that the parents of aggressive children hold.

It is axiomatic that the behaviour of individuals in a social context is governed by a set of beliefs and social attitudes which are linked to the requirements society has for the conduct of individuals. The beliefs and attitudes held by parents are mirrored in their behaviour which is there to be observed and so becomes the template for their children's own social and anti-social behaviour. The mothers of aggressive children are shown to hold beliefs about social development that are considerably different from the beliefs held by mothers whose children are not aggressive and who appear to be learning normal social behaviours (Rubin and Mills, 1992). The mothers of aggressive children appear to believe very much in a 'Do as I say, not as I do' philosophy and use this as the basis for direct and aggressive teaching. They are less willing than the mothers of non-aggressive children to allow any degree of negotiation or experimentation from their children and so stifle opportunities to consider alternative perspectives or to reflect on the consequences of various styles of interactive behaviour for others as well as themselves. Thus, these mothers expected their children to 'Do as they were told' with no further teaching or modelling (Siegel, 1982). This style of social teaching is doomed to failure and is associated with later poor development of interpersonal problem-solving skills (McGillicuddy-de Lisi, 1982). It is, therefore, a quirk of human nature that parents who believe their children should learn social skills in this way are the ones most likely to have children who fail to learn the desired lessons.

It is paradoxical that, despite their belief in telling children what they should do, the mothers of aggressive pre-school children often choose indirect strategies or no strategies at all in order to deal with unacceptably aggressive behaviour from their children, when compared with the mothers of non-aggressive children. Outside of the home, the mothers of the aggressive children are less likely to adopt consistent strategies for managing the aggression despite the fact that their children's behaviour makes them angry. Thus there is a pronounced disparity between the rigidity of their direct lessons and their actual parenting style which may be described as *laissez-faire*. In the writer's experience this can be explained by the fact that many of these mothers are visibly intimidated by their own children. They are both angered and frightened by them and frequently allow aggressive behaviour that is socially unacceptable to continue rather than risk the wrath of the child. Such parents often console themselves with little idioms such as 'He's going through a phase' and use these phrases as an excuse for non-confrontational strategies that are designed simply to keep the peace. It is inevitable that nursery and play group staff see such inconsistent styles of management breaking down and merely perpetuating high levels of aggression (Patterson, 1986). It is particularly tragic when parents use the concept of phases or some other mythical explanation such as diet or additives to explain their children's aggression and, in so doing, absolve themselves of all responsibility for it.

Inevitably, continued exposure to the aggression of their children brings about a degree of habituation such that the mothers become used to it and experience less surprise and anxiety about it. This is in direct contrast to the mothers of children who are not normally aggressive who are shocked and alarmed when their children do show aggression; this leads them to take effective action.

A further complexity often arises when the child enters compulsory education. As the aggressive behaviour continues into infant education so the mothers of aggressive children are more likely than most to be confronted by teachers and head teachers, other parents and a variety of other adults all complaining about attacks made on other children. The fear of criticism and reprimand from other adults is often greater than the intimidation they feel from their children and the mothers are then likely to respond in a highly punitive way, contrasting greatly with the *laissez-faire* styles they have previously adopted. In the writer's experience, they seek all sorts of false explanations, in which they may genuinely believe, to explain the behaviour of their children, often seeking to blame other children's influences, their own children's 'biology' or even the weather in order to avoid thinking of themselves as failed parents.

Parental behaviour as a model for children's aggression

If parental beliefs are associated with aggression then it is probable that their own behaviour is even more likely to be a direct antecedent of aggressive behaviour in their children. As has been mentioned above, the belief system of parents has direct influence on their behaviours such that faulty beliefs about the role and severity of aggression are likely to be reflected in the parents' own anti-social behaviour.

There are significant differences between the management styles of the parents of aggressive children and parents whose children are not aggressive. Baumrind (1971) produced a useful model for parenting styles which this writer has found useful for conceptualising the impact of parental models on the development of pro-social behaviour in young children. Her model portrays parenting styles on two dimensions – *warmth-responsive* and *control-demandingness*. The first dimension conceptualises a continuum for the *affective* nature of parenting; thus at one end it has warmth and sensitive behaviour directed at the child, at the other end the characteristics of the behaviour are coldness or even hostility. The second dimension is a continuum of *power-assertion*. At one end of this continuum is an absence of power assertiveness; the parent capitulates to the child's impulsive and egocentric demands and provides little or no supervision and little or no control. The child is in control and the parent is powerless. At the other end of the continuum the parent shows entirely opposite characteristics, power assertiveness is manifest in rigid, demanding parental behaviour enforced by painful sanctions and other excessive controls. In the middle of this continuum, the parent most likely to promote adequate pro-social development uses power-assertive methods when necessary, sparingly and consistently, whilst also making sure that the child is encouraged through praise and affection towards normal acceptable behaviours. Although simplistic, it is possible to conceive of these two dimensions interacting and enabling a fourfold description of parenting based on characteristic behaviours at or between the two extremes of the two continua. Thus Baumrind describes parental styles that include:

- *authoritative parenting* characterised by high warmth and high control,
- *authoritarian parenting* characterised by low warmth and high control,
- *indulgent/permissive parenting* based on high warmth and low control, and
- *indifferent/uninvolved parenting* showing low warmth and low control. (Baumrind, 1971)

Children respond to these four different styles of parenting by producing different behavioural outcomes. Thus, children subject to the authoritative/democratic parenting style tend to develop mature pro-social behaviour and successful moral reasoning. Their self-esteem tends to be high and they are usually socially responsible, competent, friendly and empathetic. They co-operate well with their peers and seem generally happy in their major environments of home and school. Steinberg *et al.* (1992) showed that such children do well academically at school. Unfortunately, however, those parents whose style is imbalanced in terms of responsiveness and control, who are authoritarian but permissive or uninvolved, are presiding over the antecedents to aggression and social incompetence (Lamborn *et al.*, 1991).

For example, parental rejection is frequently associated with early childhood aggression. Rejecting parents are more likely than most to apply power-assertive strategies, including physical punishment. Those who are particularly cold and rejecting towards their children, make use of strong physical punishments and deliver inconsistent discipline. They are far more likely to create aggressive pre-school children than other parents (Conger *et al.*, 1992). Similarly Weiss *et al.* (1992) showed that harsh parental discipline was an extremely good predictor of childhood aggression in school. The mechanism by which parental hostility and rejection gives rise to childhood aggression seems fairly simple. Firstly, this style gives rise to a family environment tainted by frustration amongst its members. This often results in expressions of anger and hostility which, if left unresolved, are likely to produce hostile and aggressive inter-personal relationships for parents and their children. Secondly, punishment associated with parental rejection provides a distinctive model of hostility and an inappropriate use of aggression to secure one's own ends (Bandura, 1977). Lastly, it is also probable that such rejection may lead to an 'internal working model' held by children in which they characterise themselves as unworthy and living in a social world that is both untrustworthy and hostile (Bowlby, 1973). Such negative perspectives easily contribute to a child's lack of empathy for others and the development of an increasingly refined aggressive behaviour repertoire which is as likely to include bullying as any other form of aggression.

There is, however, one complication in this apparently simple process that gives rise to childhood aggression. Parke and Slaby (1983) noted that the parents of aggressive children are not always cold and punitive towards these children. Rather, they may be inconsistent, under some circumstances applying power-assertive strategies and in others actually encouraging the behaviour that they have at other times tried to suppress. Thus these parents may strongly punish a child for showing aggression within the home but may actually reinforce it when it occurs within the peer group outside the home. Patterson (1982) is amongst researchers who have suggested that some parents gain vicarious reinforcement when their children are able to dominate their peer group, through the use of aggression. Such parents often fail to support school-teachers' attempts to modify that aggression, even though they are punitive of it within the home situation.

Permissiveness of aggression is important within the other extreme of parenting style as well. This is parental over-permissiveness which is characterised by indulgence and general lack of supervision, such that aggressive behaviour is tolerated in situations where the child gains positive reinforcement for behaving in that way. Thus, Olweus (1980) reported that maternal permissiveness of aggression was the *best* predictor of childhood aggression.

Influences on parenting styles

The preceding observations demonstrate that many pre-school children who become aggressive have parents who are rejecting, neglectful, sometimes over-protecting and frequently users of inconsistent disciplinary strategies that are characterised by power-assertive methods. It is important that we understand why parents respond to their children in these ways if we are to be able to provide effective intervention strategies that reverse the trends and so help young children to develop better pro-social skills. It is not sufficient merely to consider these parents as incompetent or lazy, as many experienced very poor parenting themselves when they were children. The complex cycles of parenting characteristics that are evident as inter-generational defects within families need to be understood in detail if they are to be broken. There is a wide range of influences that appear to be antecedents to negativity in child rearing and many parents respond in ways which contribute to their child's later aggressive conduct disorder.

The characteristics of children are well known to be associated with the ways in which parents respond to them. Thus they respond differently to children who are perceived to be 'easy', 'wary' or 'difficult' (e.g., Lytton, 1990). Other researchers conclude that parenting emotions, beliefs, cognitive events and behaviours must be viewed within the spectrum of variables that include family resources, experiences during the life course of the parents, the quality of the parents' relationship and the level of support they enjoy within their social network (e.g., Cox et al., 1989).

Stress and parenting. The association between the experiencing by parents of stress, coupled with a lack of social support, is well known to reduce the quality and effectiveness of their parenting style. Economic stress, whether it be brought on by poverty or bad management, invariably brings feelings of frustration, anger, helplessness and resentment which may lead to irritability in parenting style. Weiss et al. (1992) demonstrated that stressful financial situations make good predictors of inconsistency, negativism and frustration shown by parents towards their children. These parents tend to be more irritable, have mood swings and show a generally lower level of tolerance for normal childhood mischievousness than is the case for parents who have no financial problems. In addition, the financially insecure parent is quite likely to be less involved with children's activities, self-centred rather than child-centred and inconsistent in the degree of nurturing they offer, compared with those parents who are financially secure (Patterson, 1986). It is these parenting behaviours, of course, that we have seen to be antecedents to the development of poor social skills in children and weakened inhibitions on aggression. It is not surprising, therefore, that many researchers report a strong positive association between children's poorly-inhibited social behaviour characterised by aggression and parental economic stress (e.g., Dooley and Catalano, 1988; Windle, 1992).

Domestic conflict. Domestic conflict or conflict between parents is a stressor that is also highly predictive of the parenting behaviour that is associated with pre-school child behaviour problems, including aggression. Unhappiness between parents is associated with negative attitudes to child rearing and is also associated with unresponsive parenting behaviours (Jouriles et al., 1991). These parenting behaviours are antecedents to aggression in childhood and hostility between parents, perhaps leading to domestic violence; they provide children with exactly the kinds of aggressive behaviour that are known to reinforce aggression outside the home. Jouriles *et al.* (1991) reported that child aggression is predicted by hostility expressed between the parents and its effects influence boys rather more than girls (see also Block, Block and Morrison, 1981).

Parent psychopathology. This is a further variable producing stress within families and is associated with maladaptive behaviour from young children, including aggression. Maternal deprivation, for example, is sometimes the cause of parental non-involvement and poor responsivity to children and has a negative impact on spontaneity for fun and general emotional support to children (Downey and Coyne, 1990). Depression in fathers can also produce poor parenting responses but depression for any family member is likely to reduce cohesion and positive emotional expression within the family group. In addition, when the depressed parent does begin to take control of his or her life again, authoritarian and punitive disciplinary measures may increase. This is often inconsistent and models the kinds of aggression that children should be learning to inhibit.

Social support. A study by Jennings *et al.* (1991) into the issue of social support demonstrated that mothers who were satisfied with their personal social support networks were more likely to find their children praiseworthy and less likely to adopt power-assertive strategies for behaviour management. It is clear that having good or at least adequate social support networks improves a parent's sense of psychological well-being and reduces frustration and insecurity. This, in turn, is reflected in the quality of the parents' interpersonal relationships, such that their contentment 'rubs off' on their children. Biological mechanisms and neurological impairments also act on children's inhibition of aggression, although such children seldom become bullies in the writer's experience.

The pathway to bullying from the pre-school years

Aggressive pre-school children are often very hard to cope with at home and within the nursery. By the time they reach primary education they have already learned that aggressive acts such as pushing, shoving and snatching are ideal for satisfying their short-term needs and objectives. The following case study provides a case in point.

> John was one of three children with strongly punitive and rather rejecting parents. He experienced considerable variation in the quality of contact with his mother and father who tended to prefer his older sister. His older brother was very aggressive towards him and often used to 'bully' him whilst his father laughed.

At the age of four he was excluded from a play group and subsequently entered an LEA nursery. Within three weeks his name had been entered in the incident log 12 times for various acts of aggression. Later he was excluded from his primary school on seven occasions because of bullying and spent two terms in a unit for disaffected pupils.

When he was 14 one of his victims, a 13-year-old boy, Tony, took an overdose of paracetamol because of the bullying by John and his unpleasant gang. Although Tony survived he suffered internal damage and was away from school for over six months. John was genuinely devastated by this outcome and repeatedly told teachers and a psychologist that he never really hurt other kids, he just frightened them.

Those of us who have worked extensively with bullies are used to hearing this last sentiment expressed. Indeed, some studies of adult bullying have heard similar puzzled comments from bullying adults (Randall, 1997), suggesting that some, perhaps many, bullies are well into adulthood before they make a link between their bullying activity and the painful feelings of their victims.

This phenomenon is so frequent a finding that there should be an attempt to explain it. It is not sufficient simply to describe the antecedents of bullying that lie in poor or different parenting; it is necessary to uncover the cognitive processes which are failing so that aggression is not properly channelled. One model that has predictive value for these bullies is that of 'Theory of Mind'. This model may also help us find more effective strategies for dealing with young school-aged children who are developing the roots of bullying behaviour.

Theory of Mind and the faulty perceptions of bullies

Given that the frequent experience of those who work with bullies is that they seem not to be able to understand the harm they are causing and genuinely believe 'We were only joking', it seems reasonable to seek an explanation for their behaviour in the ways in which they are able to conceptualise their social interactions. Many seem to have no significant awareness of the extent to which their victims feel an injuring anxiety, shame and helplessness. In the writer's experience, many believe that the effects of the bullying upon their victims only last as long as each incident.

This type of naivity cannot simply be interpreted in terms of the bullies' intellectual prowess, or lack of it. Although empathy is an intellectual activity, it is certainly not restricted to those of average intelligence or above and, as in the case study above, many of the bullies that appear to have this faulty understanding of the impact of their actions are certainly not intellectually impaired.

There has been significant interest in children's understanding of their own mental states and those of others over a wide range of psychological fields of study. This has come to be known as 'Theory of Mind' and it is of interest to researchers working with children having developmental disorders such as autism (Baron-Cohen, 1989) and those working with children having significant social problems (e.g., Steerneman et al., 1996). The term 'Theory of Mind' seems first to have been used by Premack and Woodruff (1978) to refer to children's ability to ascribe thoughts, ideas, intentions, feelings and beliefs to other people and then to use this knowledge either to predict or to manipulate the behaviour of others.

The identification of emotions and theory of mind are seen as complementary activities (e.g., Steerneman et al., 1996) in that the recognition of emotions in oneself and others is the ability to interpret one's own mental behaviour and that of others in particular contexts. In fact the ability to recognise emotions can be seen as fundamental to a developed theory of mind and it is for this reason that Baron-Cohen and other researchers believe that developmental disorders such as autism are characterised by an inability to use theory of mind to develop the understanding of other people's feelings that becomes empathy. Children can only place themselves in the situation of others if they have developed their own theory of mind and understand that everyone has a unique 'mind' which is different from their own but which nevertheless can experience a full range of emotions. Thus the possession of a theory of mind enables children to give meaning to social behaviour and to modify their behaviour according to their beliefs about how observers are receiving it. Such social insight and understanding of the social environment obviously have much to do with skilled social behaviour and it is probable that many bullies who do not fully understand the consequence of their actions upon their victims, may lack the skill.

Not surprisingly, children's capacity to put themselves in the position of others is partly dependent on the quality and quantity of their interactions with others, particularly their parents. These are as important as the social cognitions of the children themselves (Dunn, 1994). Since parents and other primary carers have a major impact on the quality of a child's social cognitions, as has been demonstrated above in relation to aggression, it is therefore obvious that children's pre-school experiences with their parents will have a profound influence on their development of theory of mind. It is likely, therefore, that those children who fail to establish an adequate theory of mind will not be able to understand the impact of their bullying behaviour upon victims.

Steerneman *et al.* (1996) propose activities for training 'theory of mind' functions for children up to eight years of age. These activities, which help them to use perceptual, affective and cognitive skills to assess the behaviour and feelings of others, appear to be suitable for use with young children who show repeated aggressive behaviour to secure their own ends. The examples given include:

- The use of screens to prevent children in the training group from seeing each other so that they can be asked to imagine what each other might be seeing of materials presented by the trainer. This kind of activity has its roots in the work of Piaget on egocentricity and is useful in teaching children gradually how to assess the perspectives of other people.
- Pictures of animals are placed in different positions and the children are asked to describe what each animal sees. In this way greater abstraction is brought to the training on perspective taking.
- Board games, such as Snakes and Ladders™, are used, and the children, one at a time, are given misleading situations that confuse them. Their feelings are examined. Some of the situations are acted-out in role play, video-recorded and analysed in subsequent sessions.
- Handpuppets are used to depict certain characters who then discuss issues like ' I think that child is sick': the children are required to join in the conversation and to focus on the cues which may have led to the idea being discussed. It would be perfectly possible to introduce 'I think that child hurts because she/he has been bullied'.
- Increasingly complex scenarios can be introduced by the puppets and later in storytelling and the children are required to give more and more detail for each one about how the characters are thinking and feeling. The pain of being bullied is an obvious target for discussion and analysis, with the children being encouraged to role play the parts of bully and victim. The long-term effects of being bullied could be focused upon as the stories about victims unfold.

There is insufficient space here to describe this training in greater detail but it is clear from the results that the researchers present that it can be effective. Such training may have much to offer teachers and others working with aggressive young bullies-in-the-making and may help to offset poor social learning experiences.

Chapter 2

Working with parents to manage children's behaviour

Alwyn Morgan and Jackie Piccos

In order to appreciate the context in which the initiative outlined in this chapter developed, it is necessary to be aware of the following factors.

In 1988, Kingston upon Hull schools were reorganised in response to dramatically falling rolls. One outcome of this exercise was to allocate home–school liaison teachers to 40 primary schools in the less-advantaged areas of the City. It was felt that if teachers and parents worked together effectively, this would bring many benefits to all concerned, including an impact on standards of attainment.

The initiative outlined in this chapter comes from one such school, which is situated on an urban post-war estate on the fringe of the City. Unemployment is far above the national average, especially amongst the male population. Drug usage, particularly that relating to a needle culture, is endemic and crimes of theft and burglary are correspondingly numerous. Vandalism is also a constant problem. Not surprisingly, the school faces a major challenge in raising the horizons of expectancy and achievement of both pupils and parents. A new head teacher was appointed in 1994. Involving parents in their children's education was an active issue for the school under the former and present head.

Local Management of Schools (LMS) introduced the concept of parents as clients, whilst OFSTED inspections gave rise to the notion of parents as consultants on the effectiveness of schools. Moreover, the publication of information on the performance of schools has introduced greater accountability to parents. The new Special Needs Code of Practice (DfE, 1994b) introduces the role of parent as advocate for the child. However, most importantly, there have been interesting developments around the significance of parents as co-educators of their children.

Subsequently, many educationists and parents across the country have been working towards what Sir Ron Dearing claims to be a 'shared responsibility' for children's education (Dearing, 1994). Working with parents should therefore currently be regarded as an issue for all teachers, irrespective of the nature of their catchment areas. However, it is acknowledged that the nature of this work varies considerably from one school to another, depending on needs, interests and resources.

Finally, it was against this backcloth that local and national concerns developed around the growth of children's challenging behaviour (including bullying), both in and out of school. This is a much debated issue which generally identifies 'parenting skills', or the perceived lack of them, as a root cause of the problem. Discussions often focus upon by whom, how, when and at what stage in life this matter should be addressed, and resourcing this work adequately is another significant concern. In the meantime, isolated and small-scale responses have been instigated by caring organisations and establishments from both the statutory and voluntary sector. Committed and visionary individuals have perceived a real need and then with limited resources established innovative practice. Some of these initiatives have deliberately avoided a 'parenting skills' label, while some have been specifically 'anti-bullying' projects. Often their success has relied heavily on the goodwill and commitment of those involved and colleagues of those involved have often questioned whether it is their responsibility to get involved with work of this nature. For instance, policemen and teachers have often stated that they should not involve themselves in what may be perceived to be social work – they have other more pressing duties! The importance of work on parenting skills and anti-bullying initiatives has therefore yet to be acknowledged as a priority for many of the organisations involved. They are still in the realms of 'it must be someone else's job'.

What follows is an account of a school that did not duck this issue and demonstrated that schools, supported by other agencies, have a key role to play in working with parents to manage children's behaviour. After all, schools generally and individual teachers become major beneficiaries from improved pupil behaviour and enhanced working relationships with parents.

The newly appointed head of the school concerned inherited a behaviour policy supported by sanctions that were not of his choosing – 'sin bins', missed playtimes, and persistent offenders spending a large proportion of the school day banished from classrooms, listening outside the door. The school nurse once commented that she despaired of seeing faces moping in cloakrooms or outside the school office and hearing despondent teachers counting the weeks until they handed pupils over either to their next class or to the secondary school. Short-term solutions may have eased the problems of the day but did little to resolve the long-term problems of bullying and persistent disruptive behaviour.

Over the next year, measures were adopted to address unacceptable behaviour, namely:

- considerable in-service training for teaching and non-teaching staff, including dinner supervisors
- a whole-school behaviour policy with parents consulted in its writing and launch
- a structured, recognised system of rewards and sanctions emphasising positive rather than negative aspects of behaviour
- frequent contact between the Head and parents of certain children, exchanging information and negotiating and designing behavioural contracts
- the provision of a mobile crèche to encourage the involvement of parents in school either as volunteer helpers or for daytime adult education classes
- renewed enthusiasm and commitment for the school's parental involvement strategy, stimulated by a newly appointed deputy head
- careful review of curricular arrangements for children with disruptive or behavioural problems
- the development of lunch-time and after school clubs and societies
- the establishment of an internal communications and incident reporting system
- the provision to parents of higher quality information about the school.

During this period, parent governors displayed increasing involvement in the school, while the school nurse and special needs co-ordinator found themselves spending more time with individual parents who were requesting advice for managing their children's behaviour at home and school. The most common issues included bullying, aggressive and destructive behaviour, swearing, bedwetting, soiling, sibling rivalry, bedtime routines, and non-compliance with parents' requests. Both came to the opinion that the parents' needs would be better met by establishing a support group for parents with some structured input, but where parents could help each other, share experiences and explore their own solutions.

When the group was established, the issues discussed became much broader with the 'management of behaviour' being only one aspect of what developed into a 'parenting skills' support group. The special needs co-ordinator, a prime mover behind this initiative, had a non-teaching commitment which provided her with time to undertake the necessary research and development work.

Establishing the group

One of the first tasks was to seek advice from people with experience in this area of work – locally from a community mental health nurse and a health visitor who had run a similar programme on another large council estate in the City; and nationally with people involved in similar schemes. This was followed by a multi-disciplinary meeting to share ideas and explore a way forward. It was decided to purchase the *Veritas Parenting Programme* (Michael and Terri Quinn, 1987) as the basis for the support group's work – the two co-ordinators (the SENCO and school nurse) modestly believing that their lack of experience called for some back-up resource materials, bought with a small grant from the LEA.

The programme

Much of the examined support material from the various sources was similar in content, whether designed for parenting skills generally, or focused specifically on bullying and difficult behaviour. It was essentially skills-based, rather than issue-based, requiring much discussion work, the participants to practise a particular skill each week, and then report back to the group.

Throughout the programme it was stressed that there were no 'right' answers. Each family had to choose what was effective for them, what worked with their children to get the desired behaviour pattern. On reflection, the overall aim was to enhance the level of communication with their children. This was often the key factor in improving discipline, getting along better, winning co-operation and giving and gaining respect.

Parents also needed to accept that if they expected their children to change, they also had to be prepared to do so themselves. This proved to be the determining factor for the value parents placed on the group.

The programme covered the following issues:

* attention-seeking behaviour – how this is unwittingly often rewarded

- making time to give your children 'good attention'
- avoiding confrontation and power struggles
- encouraging responsibility in children – allowing them to make choices and decisions, making it safe for them to make mistakes, encouraging independence, and coping with peer pressure
- giving plenty of realistic praise and encouragement for improvement (not empty flattery), effort, being specific and building children's self-esteem
- listening skills, especially listening for feelings, reflecting them back, trying to understand, showing empathy and respect
- problem-solving techniques, giving 'I' messages, brainstorming, getting commitment and reviewing solutions
- discipline and punishment, applying consequences, the importance of rewards, setting limits, being consistent, offering choices, setting a good example and 'time out'
- talking things out together, family meetings, co-operating and quality time together
- developing respect between family members, meeting needs, raising the family's self-esteem and increasing self-confidence
- what kind of family are we aiming for?
- parents' needs, effective parenting, our own childhood and how it shapes us as parents, and feelings of failure.

Parents were also asked how to apply particular skills to specific situations. Use was made of tapes, videos and role play. Discussions were wide-ranging, often drawing on parents' own childhood experiences. Occasionally, parents related very negative experiences from their own upbringing with which they had never dealt. This was found to be a very sensitive matter which sometimes required specialist help. This led to the need to be aware of when to refer parents to other agencies if family problems went beyond the scope of the programme.

The support group co-ordinators could not be viewed as experts, for fear of being expected to answer all questions and sort out each family in turn. The role was to convey the support material clearly, organise the group according to the syllabus and timetable, maintain confidentiality and ensure the group worked well together. The support group concluded with the parents and children being photographed together for the local newspaper.

Evaluating the effectiveness of the group

Initially, there was an element of disappointment over the fact that from the 14 parents who were approached or who expressed an interest in the group, only half of that number actually attended the first session.

Additionally, over the duration of the course, two parents dropped out. However, of those who completed the programme, the impact on the families has been profound. On more than one occasion, parents have stated that 'it has transformed my life'.

The motivation, will and capacity to change displayed by some of the parents was quite startling. Not surprisingly, those who benefited most, were the ones that worked the hardest.

The parents who dropped out may have been seeking easy solutions and were unable, for personal reasons, to commit the necessary amount of effort to effect changes in the manner in which they managed their children's behaviour.

The original hopes and expectations of those parents who completed the course, appear to have been met. When questioned at the initial meeting these included:

- to have more time for my other children
- I want a better behaved child
- to be able to control my anger
- new ideas on how to manage my child
- I want a happier child
- to get close to my children
- more understanding of my children
- to have fun with my children
- friendship with my children
- more control of my children.

At the end of the first course a questionnaire was issued to the parents. Four of the seven were returned and all without exception commented on how valuable it had been to meet other parents and share experiences. Their own feelings of confidence and self-esteem had soared and they considered themselves to be more effective and responsible parents. The teaching staff also commented on the relaxed and confident appearance of the parents.

It was also pleasing to note that the parents progressed to greater involvement in the school, as volunteer helpers in the classroom, participating in adult education courses and as parent governors. Prior to attending the support group, many expressed their anxieties about approaching the school for fear of being spoken to by teachers about the behaviour of their children!

The greatest benefit for the parents was in terms of their raised self-esteem, personal growth, and confidence in all relationships, not just with their children. The participants also empowered each other to become more confident educators of their children, thus enabling themselves to set consistent guidelines and expectations for their children's behaviour.

Some of the successes were quite astounding. One mother and her five-year-old daughter had spent considerable periods of time arguing – the little girl demanded expensive parties, clothes, shoes, computers and bedroom furniture. This resulted in the daughter spending her weekends with her grandmother and her early evenings in bed, as mother and daughter found it difficult to get on with each other. Three weeks into the course, the daughter stayed at home at the weekend and her mother baked with her and actually enjoyed the experience. The following week the father came into the school to offer his thanks for the improvement the group had made.

Whilst parents felt their children were better behaved at home, class teachers saw no such improvement in the short-term. One teacher commented that 'although it may not have solved problems in school, it has made communication with parents easier and demonstrates the need to develop a team approach to counter bullying and problem behaviour'. However, too much had been expected too soon. Eighteen months on, the children's behaviour, with one exception, is very much improved. The children now achieve awards for good behaviour and academic achievement.

Finally, both co-ordinators believe that they personally have benefited enormously. They claim that it has also helped them as parents, and to be more tolerant and understanding in a professional capacity. Most significantly they have been surprised how something so simple could have such an impact on the lives of others.

Principles that underpin good practice

A number of factors have contributed to the success of this initiative that may also influence whether or not the described practice might be initiated elsewhere.

(i) *The Headteacher*, supported by his governors, played a key role in demonstrating a clear commitment to the contribution that parents could make to their children's education and particularly in influencing behaviour modification. Such a commitment can vary quite considerably from one school to another. In some schools, heads actively acknowledge the importance of parents, whilst in others their role is seen as little more than that of fund-raisers.

The commitment of the primary school featured in this chapter is demonstrated by the fact that the support group met on a regular basis in the school staff room – an area which in many schools is regarded as a 'no go area' for parents. All too frequently, many teachers find a variety of reasons for not allowing parents anywhere near the 'hallowed' area –

'they might see or overhear something that they shouldn't', 'there's no room for them in here', etc. In this particular instance, the weekly support group meetings were held from the start of the school day until break time, and staff would wait until the session was finished before walking in for their mid-morning tea or coffee. The subsequent interaction between parents and teachers over the break contributed greatly to the general quality of home–school links at the school.

(ii) *A whole-school approach to working with parents was encouraged.* An effective home–school liaison strategy necessitates a commitment that embraces teaching and non-teaching staff. Parents need to know that they are welcomed and valued by all concerned and not simply by one teacher who may have a specific responsibility for the work. The whole-school approach was undoubtedly reflected in the ethos of the school and through the range of initiatives that were encouraged to involve parents actively in their children's education. It was also reinforced by a school policy statement.

(iii) Having advocated the importance of a whole-school approach, there is still *a need for a key person at a relatively senior level within the school to lead, manage and co-ordinate developments with parents.* Having a whole-school approach can all too easily allow staff to leave it to someone else to instigate new developments. In this particular instance the deputy head teacher had the home–school liaison responsibility, and provided support and encouragement to the special needs co-ordinator for her work with the support group.

(iv) *Training and support* is a further significant factor that generates positive relationships between home and school. Generally speaking, very few teachers have received any guidance in their initial training or INSET provision on working with parents. This may account for why certain schools continue to see parents as a peripheral issue. Teachers may lack the insight, skills and confidence to encourage the active involvement of parents. Until this matter is addressed, many teachers will be of the opinion that, because parents failed to feature as an issue in their initial training, they cannot be particularly important to current educational practice.

In Humberside there was a comprehensive range of one-day training courses for school staff and governors to explore the varied aspects of work relating to the involvement of parents in their children's education. These courses either reinforced their existing beliefs and commitment or encouraged teachers to develop new forms of practice.

Additionally, there were mutual support group meetings for teachers and workers from other agencies who were involved with parenting skills groups. Experiences and ideas were exchanged, and all concerned reflected upon their practice and challenges. These sessions proved to be invaluable, particularly as at the time such initiatives were relatively innovative.

School-based training or talks to staff meetings were also offered. The latter proved to be a useful means for the staff at the school concerned to appreciate the value and importance of their parenting skills support group.

(v) *Inter-agency collaboration,* as identified earlier, was a further essential element in the success of the parent support group. Parenting skills are not solely an issue for schools. This is also a developing area for many agencies in the voluntary and statutory sectors where the focus may be on the pre-school sector, health matters, social work, youth work, law and order, the church or adult education. Many of these agencies have demonstrated a commitment to parenting skills work and behaviour modification. It is therefore advantageous for schools and other agencies to work collaboratively around common issues. Individual services may bring about change, but when agencies work together, the outcome can be far more effective.

(vi) Such new initiatives have *resource implications*. In this case there were two main needs. Firstly, funding to purchase the research information and support materials that would underpin the programme. More importantly, the special needs co-ordinator was released from her teaching duties, not simply to lead the group, but to undertake the necessary planning, home visits, contact with other agencies and any follow-up work. This was a clear demonstration of the value that the school placed on parents.

It should also be made clear that the workload for the co-ordinators was particularly heavy, in preparation time, as well as leading sessions. Time was needed to familiarise other staff with the aims and content of the package, and to encourage parents to support the initiative. Atkin, Bastiani and Goode (1988) state: 'Working with parents takes time, energy and commitment; producing materials to support such work needs all of these and financial resources as well'. This work cannot be encouraged solely by appealing to the goodwill of interested parties.

(vii) The establishment of this parent support group was *a response to a real and articulated need.* Both parents and teachers acknowledged this and were prepared to do something about it. It is pointless a school perceiving it to be a need and deciding that it would be good for the parents. There must be common agreement on the value of an exercise of this nature by both parties. This in turn should also apply to the 'curriculum', which should be negotiated with the group.

(viii) *Personal contact with parents* proved to be the most effective means of establishing the group. This entailed approaching parents either in school or at home. However, it is sometimes difficult for parents to acknowledge that they have a problem and need help, particularly from a school. It can also be hard for them to find the time, energy and will-power to carry through the necessary changes.

It is also suggested that parents with children in either school-based pre-school provision, nursery and/or reception classes be targeted in the first instance. This is where the greatest opportunities for personal contact lie. Additionally, it capitalises on the potential for change before problems and negative relationships get too entrenched. If effective links with parents can be established in the early years of children's education, the challenge for teachers in the remaining phases of education will be to build upon these new working relationships.

Leaflets and posters were relatively ineffective in generating the necessary level of interest. However, they served the purpose of conveying a message regarding the school's willingness to work with the parents to bring about change in children's behaviour.

(ix) *The skills of the co-ordinators* were also key factors in the development of the group. Their commitment and empathy brought its rewards. Other qualities are listed by Wolfendale (1986), for example: 'listening skills, eliciting information, facilitating and sustaining conversation, keeping on the subject, being supportive, positive yet realistic, conveying and representing school policy, counselling, etc'. Participants in this work should attempt not to appear over-judgemental.

(x) *Working through a structured programme helped the leaders.* It was helpful to be aware of all the materials that could be utilised, before negotiating and agreeing on a course of study with the parents.

(xi) *The co-ordinators accepted that they were not doing it solely for the children.* With an initiative of this nature, parents can develop quite significantly. Be prepared to see some of them outgrow the group and move on to other initiatives or employment. This was the case with the majority of the first cohort of parents, who in turn have become strong advocates for the school. It might also be possible to identify future leaders for further support groups from amongst their number.

Although the original aim was to improve children's behaviour, the increased confidence and self-esteem of parents became the first significant outcome. This undoubtedly in turn brought its rewards, as outlined by Campion (1993): 'children pick up messages which suggest whether their carers are respected and valued by others and this directly affects their self-esteem. Children who grow up with carers who have the respect of those around them are likely to feel good about themselves.'

(xii) In order to make the group accessible to parents, *it was essential to provide crèche provision* for those with pre-school children. This service should also be an essential part of all home–school activities, whether during or after school hours.

(xiii) *Consideration should be given to follow up meetings, to maintain the newly established practices.* Studies, including that of Sutton (1992), acknowledge that parents can slip back into old habits of being inconsistent, making threats or promises, or forgetting to commend and encourage children in the desired behaviour. It is important that schools should not abandon parents just at the point where they are wanting to develop. Some possibilities are:

- monthly self-help group meetings
- 'one off' meetings to consider specific topics in some depth
- parents networking other established groups locally and further afield
- family/community initiatives, events, days, organised by the school or group
- family fun homework challenges which contribute to enhanced communication between the parent/carer and children. These entail calling upon a parent or older person to assist a child with a specific task or challenge relating to school work. These need to be non-threatening activities that enable parents of any background or ability to help. Most importantly the activities have to be fun! This approach is an extension of home–school reading into any area of the school curriculum at either primary or lower secondary level.

(xiv) A rewarding development is to *record the child's behaviour before, during and after the programme.* This is an integral part of Sutton's programme (1992) and a natural extension of the approach adopted for individual programmes in most schools. Scores are calculated for specific compliant and non-compliant behaviour so that any improvement can be pinpointed and recorded.

(xv) Finally, it should always be remembered that *there are also disappointments in this work and, more often than not, expectations, particularly from colleagues, can be unrealistic.* In this particular instance there was an initial expectancy of immediate changes in pupil behaviour. Although this failed to materialise, the long-term benefits have been considerable. When developing improved working relationships with parents, success is always measured in very small advances and slow stages.

Challenges to be addressed

Two major challenges need to be faced. Firstly, the importance of parenting skills work has yet to be acknowledged by the major policy makers. Unfortunately, an alternative regressive approach appears to be in vogue, as in retrospective retribution directed at parents. This is reflected in the growing debate over the virtues of the American practice of fining parents for the misbehaviour of their children, whilst schools are attempting to make increased use of home–school contracts to enforce parental support for their children's schooling. Neither of these measures seems to offer long-term solutions to the problems of weak parenting.

To date in the UK, parenting skills work and anti-bullying projects have largely been developed over and above the other general responsibilities of the organisations concerned. However, their very limited resources have been committed to these isolated initiatives because they know it works and brings untold benefits.

There is undoubtedly a need for these piecemeal and unco-ordinated developments to be researched. This might then prove once and for all the essential nature of this work. It would appear that virtually little or no local or central government funding has been accorded to support and encourage such developments. At a time when there appears to be a desperate need to expand support of this nature, there appears to be either a lack of understanding, commitment or vision to empower parents to take more control of their own lives.

Secondly, this work will only be taken seriously if it is resourced adequately. Sadly, the considerable financial constraints placed on schools in recent years have seen many resources allocated away from work with parents. This has certainly been the case in the former Humberside schools. In the current restrictive climate, the way forward might therefore call for the redistribution of resources away from reactive measures that reinforce feelings of inadequacy and failure in parents, to positive, proactive initiatives that enhance confidence and well-being in the future generation of parents.

Will anyone respond to these challenges?

Chapter 3

'Bully 4 U':
a community approach to bullying

Louise Warner and Martin Richards

Children live in a world of play. If we are to reach them so that they can learn to make decisions about how they behave and choose how to relate to others, then the medium of play is a worthwhile approach. Children live in communities – of which schools are only a part, even though a significant part. The power differences and bullying behaviour that have been extensively researched in schools are also present throughout communities. We have adopted a community approach to anti-bullying work using the medium of play, drama, physical movement, dance and other creative methods. We wish to describe how a small-scale community-based project evolved and the underlying principles which guided our work.

The Project is based within West Leeds Family Service Unit – a neighbourhood centre which offers a range of services focused on supporting families with young children (e.g. play group, Drop-In, adult groups that are dealing with issues such as domestic violence and racial harassment). The Unit offers services within a local geographic area. The staff group is striving to avoid labelling families or individuals as problems – rather it adopts an approach that seeks to promote confidence and to encourage people to take control of their lives. There is a clear recognition of the difficulties of living in an inner-city, materially-deprived environment and the Unit seeks to reduce the impact of society's structural stresses on local families. One of the services offered to the community is an annual summer play scheme which became the catalyst for West Leeds Family Service Unit to become involved in anti-bullying work.

The play scheme is organised for five- to 11-year-old children who live in the area. Feedback from the Summer 1994 play scheme reported that 72 per cent of those who attended expressed concerns about bullying and at times many felt frightened about the bullying that had taken place. Two of the workers involved on the play scheme heard the experiences of the local children who described bullying in a variety of contexts: at school, on the street, at home, in recreational groups. Bullying was not a whole school affair but a whole community affair.

This group would examine bullying and try to offer resources to local children. The group was formed by approaching children aged seven to 12 who had been on the play scheme and who lived in the streets immediately next to the Unit. We began with 12 children meeting after school one evening a week for about two hours.

We believed that in forming this group we should ensure sufficient obvious differences and variety in the group. We had male and female. We had different family structures: single father, two parent and single mother families. We ensured a cultural mix which reflected the local population: Asian, White British, Afro-Caribbean and mixed race children. When we approached children and their families to join the group we were also sensitive to their customs and beliefs. Thus, in the process of inviting sisters from the Muslim Pakistani community, we discussed with their mother what would ease their attendance. We were aware that if the sisters were invited that there would be an assumption that the invitation would be for the whole family and, therefore, we made provision for their male cousins to join. The male cousins' attendance also enhanced acceptability of the sisters belonging to a mixed sex group. In addition, once the group began we took care in the choice of activities (such as avoiding eating out together).

The worker diversity seemed to add to the group too. We had our differences in professional background, knowledge, interests, age and so on. We had differing roots and hence various skills. The limitations in having three White workers promoted an intention to widen the racial mix of the worker team. Some of these differences were obvious to the children, some emerged through the group, not least our focus on looking at differences. We used games that promoted the positive approach to difference – for example, the Applause Game.

APPLAUSE GAME

1. Group members sit in a circle.
2. Group leaders ask: 'Everyone who is ... (describing a difference, e.g. living in a flat) ... stand up'.
3. Those who are described stand whilst those seated applaud and cheer.
4. Group leaders keep asking the group the various differences within this category (e.g. house, hostel, etc.) until everyone has stood and been applauded.

In time the initial obvious differences identified by the children and ourselves, such as our clothing or hair colour, moved on to more personal aspects. We applauded our family structure, our social relationships, our roots.

We played physical games and movement games repeatedly which were built into our weekly structure. These games provided a format for us to say something about ourselves with our bodies.

Another popular game to help build confidence was the name and shape game.

NAME AND SHAPE

1. Group stand or sit in a circle.
2. A group member says their name and simultaneously makes a shape with his/her body.
3. All the group members together make the same shape and say the name with as much similar quality of movement and voice tone as possible.
4. Leader thanks the member making the shape.
5. On to each person in turn around the group.

Another game regularly played was 'The Sun Shines On' which provided an opportunity for whoever was in the centre of the circle to ask the question of the group she or he always wanted to ask. It promoted curiosity as well as bringing out the differences within the group.

THE SUN SHINES ON

1. One person in the middle with the remainder of the group sitting in a circle on chairs.
2. Person in the middle says: 'The sun shines on all those who ... ' (describe anything you want to know from the colour of socks to those who have been to a funeral).
3. Everyone to whom this applies has to stand up, move

around and find a chair, as does the person in the middle.
4. Last person remains in the middle and calls out the next 'Sun shines on all those who ... '.

With the children moving on to more personal areas and taking more risks with each other, many differences were exposed. Having reached this level of trust, it was possible to introduce role play and the management of conflict in the community.

There followed a remarkably candid display of the tensions that the children had witnessed on the streets outside the Unit. The children showed some of the behaviour that disturbed them and their emotional response to it, often anger and fear.

The first group, who decided to name the anti-bullying project 'Bully 4 U', ran weekly for three months. It became difficult to hold all the group members' attention and retain their engagement in the activities. However, despite limitations, it became possible to raise awareness about bullying, through the group members, to the local community, by the use of questionnaires both in the group and with parents, by exchanging anti-bullying materials with local schools. It became possible to look at how the children defined bullying.

The previous age range of Year 2 to Year 7 was reduced to a group for eight- to 11-year-olds. Numbers were limited to nine children partly due to our limitations of space and partly due a wish to work with greater intensity by, for example, using small subgroups. A mix of children from the first Bully 4 U group and local children new to the Project who had been identified as being bullied or bullying others joined the group. So Bully 4 U 2, the second community-based anti-bullying group evolved. This group met once a week for two hours after school had finished for a period of six months.

A game was introduced where each child is introduced in turn, another child adds a complimentary adjective, and then all group members repeat the adjective and name, e.g. 'Happy' Holly, 'Super' Shahnaz, 'Wise' Wesley. Some of the children have not found this game easy: some initially used derogatory adjectives in a jocular way. Workers maintained the focus on the child until they or another group member produced a positive description.

The 'Positive Throws' – another game often used – involved a soft ball being thrown to group members and their name and an 'I like ... ' statement accompanying the throw. A tight control had to be maintained to ensure all the comments were positive and that everyone received a throw and comment. At first, group members would make comments such as 'I like the way you played football'. However, the longer the group practised this game, statements became more individual and open: 'I like your sense of humour'. In addition, the group members came out of their subgroups; for example, boys threw to girls, saying a genuine complimentary phrase.

Once the positive games were familiar and part of the structure, the playing at the beginning of the group had an effect on the group process so that a nurturing atmosphere was promoted throughout the session. Early on, the game was embarrassing for the group; in time, the children wanted the game more and more, hungry for the compliments to be stated.

One of the aims of the Project was to offer choices to the children. The Project recognised that there were limitations that were imposed on the children due to the social, environmental and economic circumstances in their lives. Yet within these limitations, there were options. Workers pointed out that everyone had choices that they could make and explored possible consequences of the choices on offer. Children had the opportunity to recognise and increase their ability to control aspects of their lives within their own cultural context. In order to offer choices there was the need for the children to learn new skills and explore new ideas. For this to happen, the workers needed to be aware of appropriate resources such as mediation skills and the 'No Blame Approach'.

The creativity of the children was noted and this was one way to offer new ideas. For example, a variety of media was used – drawing, mask-making, acting, modelling, drama and dance. Role plays encouraged the children to think of different ways of viewing bullying incidents. One role play involved 'freeze, show us your fantasy, show us other options'. So a typical bullying scene would be played out by the children. When a role play came to a critical point, the action would be frozen and there would be an opportunity to fantasise about what you would like to do. This was encouraged in the belief that there is nothing that is so bad that you cannot show or talk about it (Gordon, 1995). The child being bullied could imagine flooring the bully or a child feeling picked on by adults could fantasise about humiliating the tormentor. After the fantasy was exposed we could then move on and think about what the child might do in her real life circumstances using the quality and the energy of the fantasy in a non-destructive way.

Part of the work in providing resources was to try to get across the ideas of 'powerless', 'power over' and 'power within' (paralleling victim, bully and assertive roles). Children often feel they are in their own powerless place when bullied, humiliated or the subject of injustice. In a school, racist name-calling situation, it may be asking what could you have done that would have retained your power but would have not got you in trouble with teachers and possibly sent home. Then look at other possibilities suggested by the group. It was exciting to see the ideas develop.

An important part of the Project was to give children their chance to solve problems rather than us adults supplying the answers. Recently, we ran an after school club based in a local school. The school has informed us that skills were used in the playground by the children: so, skills are operating in their lives rather than only in the groupwork setting.

The Project wished to work on a premise that we should not label or blame. However, there is an acceptance that at times of crisis, intervention and the prevention of continued physical or emotional hurt might be necessary. The Project was careful not to collude with bullying behaviour. It viewed bullies and victims as not being clearly defined discrete groups; the person who acted the bully role in one context, may act the victim in another and perhaps be the bystander in a third. The group's purpose was not to identify the bully or victim. The Project considered bullying as part of a whole, wider system. It recognised that children live within a variety of settings and was able to have an influence on a child's whole life. It could raise awareness of what constitutes bullying behaviour.

The range of possible behaviours and learned skills on offer to the child could be extended. These choices were transferable into the various settings in a child's life. For example, one parent complained that her previously passive daughter was now more difficult to handle in that she was questioning decisions and more assertive in the home. The changes in individuals in the group could create a 'domino effect' that offered the possibility of change in various settings.

Bully 4 U 2 began with the small group of nine children and hoped to grow into schools and into homes. In a meeting with parents, workers were informed of the community-wide prevalence of bullying. This reinforced the need to look at bullying in a systematic way. Further support for a systemic view of anti-bullying strategies came from the evaluation of the Bully 4 U 2 group. The findings included the need for heightened parent–school communication about bullying, again a concern about the interrelationship between neighbourhood and school bullying and highlighted the extent of racist name-calling and bullying both at school and on the street.

To respond to the above findings, the Project embarked on three ventures over succeeding months:

- an after school club based in one of the primary schools

- 'Kick Off', a parents' group meeting in community-based premises
- Bully 4 U 3, a community-based group meeting after school in a community setting.

This community group which included two girls who were members of the Bully 4 U 2 group, was aimed at girls of differing ethnic groups. It was set up in response to an identified local need to support girls in the transition from local junior schools to the more daunting environment of large comprehensives. There were themes for each week and we allowed something of what the children wanted to include rather than simply running our agenda.

We used the talking stick in Bully 4 U Club '3' which also offered a structure so everyone had time to be heard. Again there was an element of ritual with the whole group sitting in a circle. Everyone had the chance to hold the stick in turn. Only the person holding the stick could talk and, having spoken, they passed it on to their neighbour. If you did not want to speak, then you were requested to hold the stick for a quiet moment. This acknowledged the presence of the silent group members as well as the more verbal ones. We usually used the talking stick at the beginning of a session, bringing us together as a group. It also helped to clear minds of events and feelings that may have happened earlier in the school day.

This ritual allowed us to create a space where the children could share thoughts and feelings. The children were encouraged to speak – the adults adopting a non-blaming and non-shaming atmosphere. In time it became a little like the Speak-Outs after the Chinese Cultural Revolution when such a structure was needed to cleanse the nation. It was a similar process with bullying which has gone on for generations. We might ask why they made such a comment, or how did they think the person felt when taunted (which we might check out with the child taunted). Similarly, in the 'Kick Off' parents' group, it did not seem helpful to make parents feel guilty. If you do so, parents may well cease talking about the way they may have used power inappropriately and so block seeing other ways which could be helpful. In the Kick Off group a process of exploration took place which became very exciting.

Parents compared how they handled their children: 'Yes, this is what I do with my child.' 'Do you do this as well?' The parents found they had allies in the group, which promoted the examination of solutions and alternatives to the behaviour. The children spoke of how they themselves had bullied or had been unkind. At times, it almost felt like an absolution, a kind of confessional time. The structure of the talking stick honoured these confessions and provided the space for them to take place.

The consultation sessions provided clues and strategies on how to overcome blockages, whether they appeared to be based in the micro system of the group or the larger system of organisations and community, their resources and attitudes. The split of consultation on the anti-bullying work from the management of the Project enhanced our ability to follow the needs indicated by those children and the adults involved in the Project.

Conclusion

We have a lot of ideas and passion about how we can progress, as do the children with whom we are in contact. We used principles to empower children that originated from the social action model coupled with systemic thinking. We incorporated into our work the use of children's creativity and their own ability to solve problems, given appropriate resources. Fundamental to our way of working is the need to focus on the positives and the children's strengths, examining difference and choices, working within a clear, reliable structure and the introduction of skills to handle bullying.

Notes

1. This chapter originated from a discussion between Carol Ciplinski, Louise Warner and Martin Richards and was developed by Louise and Martin.
2. The work of the Bully 4 U Project at West Leeds Family Service Unit has been supported by funding from Leeds Safer Cities, the Joseph Rowntree Charitable Trust, the Onaway, Tudor and the Audrey and Stanley Burton (1966) Charitable Trusts.

Chapter 4

From home to school

Delwyn Tattum and Eva Tattum

Introduction

Progress from home to compulsory schooling is an event that is significant for children, for whom it means new experiences and new relationships. For some children it can be upsetting, even traumatic. The child leaves a warm, intimate and familiar place for a large, confusing, strange place. The occasion is also significant for parents as they first accompany their children to school and hand over responsibility for at least part of their children's learning and development to a professional person and a formal organisation. In fact, this process of progress into pupilhood has been called a form of social weaning. For upon entering the school for the first time the child meets a whole set of new constraints – new ways of behaving, new forms of authority, and new methods of evaluation. The child must adapt to the demands made by fresh surroundings, timetabled work and play, and a whole range of challenging relationships and behavioural expectations. And even though most children now have an opportunity to go to some form of pre-schooling, the actual entry into the infant class can still be upsetting for many. In fact, the importance of nursery-type education lies not so much in lasting academic gains but in personal and social advantages. It prepares children for full-time schooling by gradually adjusting them to being with other children, responding to relative strangers, and experiencing being in an orderly, controlled environment.

Undoubtedly, a great deal of social learning has already taken place in the home but upon entry into school more formal education takes place. One of the functions of the school is to socialise children into the 'ways of society', that is, to give the child the knowledge and skills necessary for survival in an advanced industrial society. This process, though, extends beyond literacy and numeracy, to include values, beliefs, attitudes, habits and appropriate normative behaviour. Increasingly, this aspect of the school's functions is being discussed with reference to social values, and aggressive and abusive behaviour as presented in disruptive behaviour and bullying.

Peer relationships and friendships

As children develop socially they deal more frequently with those who make up their growing social world. They form relationships with adults beyond their immediate family and play with other children. They come to understand now others affect them and they, in turn, affect the behaviour of others. As the child progresses through primary school, friends become more and more important. They are important sources of companionship and recreation, someone with whom you share advice and valued possessions, are confidantes, critics and allies and provide support in times of stress and worries. By the final year of primary school, ten-year-olds consider friendship to be a sharing of inner thoughts and feelings. They understand that a friend is a special person with whom you can enjoy mutual respect and affection. In this way children realise that acts of friendship could change a person's feelings from lonely and sad to being wanted and happy – as is the case with many victims of bullying. One of the most reassuring bulwarks against the bully is to be part of a close friendship or friendship group.

It is possible that peer relationships play an even more important role today than in the past. The increasing number of working mothers and one-parent families has resulted in earlier entry of young children into organised peer group settings such as day care centres and nursery schools. Furthermore, children today participate more frequently in out of school activities and organised leisure activities. These experiences guarantee that children spend considerable time with same age peers throughout childhood. Therefore, it is very important that a child enjoys close relationships and learns the social skills necessary to negotiate successful entry into the various social worlds available. Children operate in two social worlds, that of child–adult relationships and then the world of peer relations.

In their relations with friends and peers the importance of perspective taking cannot be over-emphasised as one of the social skills young children need to learn and in that respect schools are especially able to provide such learning opportunities. As far as bullying is concerned, young children need to be introduced to seeing the act of bullying from the victim's viewpoint and, hence, show them more sympathy and support.

Davies (1982) suggests that in addition to having 'best friends' a child may also have 'contingency friends' to turn to in case their closest friend is not available. She regards a friend as someone who was sensible and loyal, who knew how to co-operate and who would share their personal world with you. With a friend the relationship is on an equal basis and provides a basic sense of security. Frowned upon behaviour included 'showing-off', because that aims to elevate the person and put you down. 'Teasing' too can upset the feeling of security, whilst for older pupils, not 'splitting' or grassing was an important rule in their code of honour. This latter point partly explains why children are unwilling to tell on classmates who bully, even though they may disapprove of or be on the receiving end of a bully's aggression.

Within the literature on peer relations there has been increasing recognition that friendship and overall group acceptance may constitute distinct and independent aspects of a child's social world. Rubin (1980) warned against the uncritical promotion of popularity as a desirable end in itself, as it may result in an emphasis on superficial relationships and unhealthy competition. Children who are not popular may well have close rewarding friendships with one or two others, whilst a child who is popular may lack one close, intimate friend and the benefits that may come from higher quality peer relationships. For example, research by McGuire and Weisz (1982) indicates a relationship between having a close friend and greater social sensitivity to the needs and feelings of others. To distinguish between the benefits of friendships and popularity carries an important message for teachers and parents, and both should seek to create opportunities for their pupils/children to interact with friends in a deep and sustained way. We are more concerned about parents who pressurise their children into having a full social diary of activities without considering the nature of the friendships which are often fleeting and insubstantial.

Schools should spell out to parents the value of their child having a close friend and encourage them to invite children in the neighbourhood to their home, not just for parties but for general play and excursions to places of interest. Equally parents should be advised to take an interest in the social life of their child in school – not just academic progress. They should talk to them about whom they play with, eat their lunch with, walk to and from school with and so on. From the school's side, teachers too should create situations which help deepen friendships. One successful scheme we have used was to get children who live close to each other to draw a plan of their route to and from school, noting names of streets, prominent buildings and other landmarks.

Play and playtime

Burns (1986) makes a distinction between 'pre-social' and 'social play'. Pre-social play of early infancy occurs when a young baby plays with inanimate objects like bells, rattles and balls which dangle from its crib – and also when the baby plays with itself, as it explores its face, fingers and toes, and sex organs.

He named three major types of social play – free play, creative play, and formal play. Physical *free play* with other children is probably the easiest for a child to engage in and is of critical importance in the socialisation process. Play fighting between peers is common from three years on through to adolescence – especially with boys. It is important for midday supervisors and teachers to recognise that play fighting can become bullying when the intent is to harm and intimidate the victim. Wrestling involves close physical contact in which each child struggles to pin his partner to the ground – in most cases it is not for real and roles are quickly reversed. Chasing play is an extension of rough-and-tumble, and the screams from an infant playground will demonstrate it is exciting and emotionally stimulating. The danger with these kinds of boisterous play is that they can become more serious in intent – especially for the most aggressive child.

Creative play is primarily pretend or fantasy play, in which a stick becomes a gun and a blanket a house. The imaginary use of inanimate objects can extend to having an imaginary companion who accompanies the child at mealtimes, in the car, to the shops and so on to bed.

Formal play involves co-operation with others in games and activities that are rule-governed. Role playing referred to above will have some rule structure but it is more likely to be particular to that single play episode. More generally applied rules come into operation at the age of six or seven years in games like tag, hopscotch, marbles and football. These are games with public rules to which all participants are expected to conform. It is important for midday supervisors to be familiar with the rules of traditional games which will then enable them to involve more children in a creative playtime activity.

Preparing for school

For most children, starting school marks the beginning of a lifetime of interest and enjoyment, involving work and play. It is an opportunity to start many new friendships, and, above all, it should be a time of fun. But arriving at a new school (play group or nursery) can also be a daunting experience and many parents are concerned whether their child will be happy. Will she or he make friends? or will the child be hurt in playground rough and tumble, or, more worrying, be bullied?

In fact, there is a lot the parents can do to assist their child to cope more easily with the demands of starting school. And whilst they may teach skills that make a child independent and capable, it is also very important that the child is also able in social and emotional skills. It is necessary, especially in large classes, to get on with other children, many of whom are strangers and from a range of home backgrounds – that is, in terms of child-rearing practices rather than socio-economic background. Some will have been taught to care and share, to join in with others and even show compassion for those people less fortunate than themselves. On the other hand, some children will come from abusive and aggressive backgrounds, where might is right and the person who is prepared to be more hurtful in what is said or done is the one who gets his or her way. And it is in school that the two extremes meet; and nothing in the experience of the former illustration will have prepared him or her to cope with the aggressive behaviour of some of their classmates. In this sense, every school provides the opportunity for bullying to take place, as children test each other out and work out their roles in classroom and playground relationships.

We asked a number of infant teachers to list the characteristics of the child who has least problems settling into school. We asked them to list them under three headings – social skills, independence skills and emotional skills. Figure 4.1 presents their responses. They are not definitive lists but provide a benchmark against which parents can prepare their children for starting school and give them the self-confidence to cope with the challenges which this new experience invariably brings.

Earlier in the chapter we indicate that young children learn bullying behaviour mainly in the home and from adults. That is, from parents or carers, or from watching television or videos unsupervised and therefore in an uncritical way. In a child's early years parents are the most influential role model. Some aggressive children are simply copying their parents. If an adult exhibits violent behaviour in the home then it is very likely that the child who witnesses it will develop his or her own aggressive streak. The danger is that the child will accept that this is normal behaviour.

Starting School		
Basic skills		Giving confidence
Social skills *Able to*	**Independence skills** *Able to*	**Emotional skills** *Able to*
Talk to other children Listen to what others have to say Share books, toys and other equipment Take turns at games Play co-operatively Accept children who are seen to be different Show sensitivity to a distressed child Wait in a queue	Put on coat without help Take shoes off and on and fasten them Keep reasonably clean and tidy Use the toilet and wash hands Move around school building and play areas Eat packed lunch or school meal Complete a task when asked to do so Concentrate on an activity for 10 to 15 minutes	Feel self-confident Control temper outbursts Talk about aggressive feelings and not hit out Control tears when things go wrong Accept reprimand from adult without becoming too upset Sit quietly in class Work and learn in co- operation with other children

Figure 4.1

In addition to socially learned behaviour a child may display uncharacteristic aggression. This may result from an inability to communicate her or his thoughts or emotions. Jealous feelings towards a new baby, for example, are common and can undermine a child's confidence in its position in the house. Finally, we cannot ignore that child abuse may result in unmanageable social behaviour, and for a school which discovers such signs of abuse there are clear guidelines for action.

Creating a safe, secure school

In the booklet *Bullying: A Positive Response* (Tattum and Herbert, 1990), guidance is provided for parents, governors and staff in schools. As part of our ongoing research we wished to develop those ideas to provide further advice for those who are responsible for the moral and social development of the under eights. To that end we consulted with parents, teachers and others, and their recommendations are briefly contained in this section and further expanded in the booklet *Bullying: The Early Years* (Tattum and Tattum, 1997).

Our starting point is that human beings are born with the natural capacity to be kind towards others. This is our optimistic view and it is supported by the research that Australian children demonstrated a basic sense of decency whereby the majority (82 per cent) expressed their disapproval of bullying behaviour. Similarly, in Toronto schools, Ziegler and Rosenstein-Manner (1991) found most children feel distressed by bullying. (For a fuller discussion of both sets of results see Tattum, 1993.) Unfortunately in the years between childhood and adulthood some children learn to behave cruelly and bully others. And as we have already discussed, this change of attitude can be learned in the home and, more significantly, it can be reinforced in schools by the way some teachers behave and the competitive climate generated in some activities. By encouraging co-operative play, teachers in nursery and infant classes can reduce the chance of bullying amongst young children. Most games played are competitive in nature and therefore have winners and losers. And whilst competitive activities such as races, board games and football encourage children to develop positive characteristics like determination, tolerance, withstanding pressure and failure, and, especially, a group feeling, they can also encourage negative qualities like aggression, selfishness and the wish to achieve regardless of others, which are the sort of feelings which can lead to bullying.

An effective way to encourage co-operation rather than confrontation is the use of role play. A group can act out a simple scenario in which some are required to help others – and then they reverse the roles. In this way play can be used to help children understand what it is like to experience bullying. Play leaders or midday supervisors can similarly encourage positive behaviour in the play area and even introduce the children to co-operative, traditional games like hopscotch and skipping.

A good way to encourage children to be responsible is to appoint 'secret friends' to quietly introduce shy or nervous children into an activity without them knowing they have been singled out for special treatment. Likewise, learning to care can come from being allocated daily tasks around the classroom. These kinds of activities and responsibilities create a caring atmosphere and teach a child how to be kind to others and not only to think of self.

In summary, we offer two presentations (Figures 4.2 and 4.3) worked out with teachers about some aims and methods of helping both the aggressive and also the vulnerable child. They illustrate a preventative approach to countering bullying by enumerating what teachers should aim to achieve in their own classrooms and some of the methods of achieving the well-being of *all* children for whom they have a duty of care.

But the work of individual teachers is most effectively achieved if it is carried out within an effective school discipline policy and programme which includes a firm stand against bullying. To this end all staff, governors, parents and children must be clear about what is

---

Helping the aggressive child
THE POTENTIAL BULLY

Aims
To get child to
  • *respect* other children
  • *respect* other creatures
  • *respect* objects (toys, books, etc)

Methods
Active listening
  • taking what she/he has to say seriously
  • no public put-downs
Create opportunities for caring and sharing
  • role play
  • circle time
  • story time
  • co-operative play
Teach idea of compassion
  • openly express compassion for others – in stories, on television,
    during play
  • convey honest emotions
Encourage respect for possessions
  • how to value and care for possessions, others' toys, school
    equipment
  • tidying up and safely storing things
Reward good behaviour
  • not just good work
  • reward words and acts of kindness, sharing and co-operation
  • show she/he is a person who is liked
Be a good model
  • by words and actions
  • kind, thoughtful
  • keep one's word

Figure 4.2

understood by bullying behaviour and that must be communicated and
discussed by all parties. Bullying takes various forms:
  • physical bullying – which needs to be distinguished from play
    fighting
  • verbal bullying can be hurtful as it can be very personal and even
    include comments about members of the family
  • hiding things can also be distressing – this form of bullying can be
    linked to stealing and threatening behaviour
  • exclusion is another form which is hurtful as phrases like, 'you're
    not coming to my party' or 'we're not playing with you', clearly
    reflect.
Finally, to achieve a whole-school policy there needs to be:

Helping the vulnerable child
THE POTENTIAL VICTIM

Aims

   To create a safe, secure environment

   To help child to make friends

   To raise self-confidence – ability to cope with new situations and persons

   To encourage sociability – helping the shy, passive, lonely or isolated child

Methods

   Actively draw the child into mixing with others

   Create structured activities – which are more reassuring than unstructured ones

   Boost self-esteem through praise, rewards and encouragement

   Suggest ways of initiating a conversation – favourite books, toys, TV programmes

   Explain that everyone feels out of things at sometime – they are *not* different

   Use role play, circle time, co-operative play to develop social skills

   Give position or jobs with responsibility

   Use more socially aware child as a 'buddy' or 'secret friend'

Figure 4.3

1. *Staff agreement* – that is, to avoid confusion all must be involved in the discussion about the need for clear rules. Rules should cover movement about the school, basic tasks and how children should behave towards each other.

2. *Consistency and coherence* – all must be acquainted with the rules and staff must diligently apply them in their classrooms, as they move about the buildings, and in the playground (see Tattum, 1986). For behind the rules are values – in other words they demonstrate to the children and others what the school stands for and believes in.

3. *Positive responses* – here we recommend that rules are emphasised in a positive rather than in a negative framework; rather, 'Try to be quiet and stay seated', in preference to, 'Don't run around making a noise'. Similarly, punishments should be non-physical, such as, removing from free-play for a short time or standing in time-out space on the playground. Staff who use aggressive methods to discipline children can only reinforce the belief that bullying is acceptable and gets the desired results.

Starting school is the most challenging experience a young child has to make in its short life, whether it be nursery or infant school. Therefore, it is important that both home and school are proactive, that is, for the former to prepare the child for the transfer and the latter by informing the family what is expected regarding behaviour and then to prepare itself to accept the child in a caring, supportive and predictable atmosphere which it has thoughtfully created. Children are entitled to expect adults to protect them from harsh and hurtful experiences, and to that end home and school should work constructively and harmoniously.

PART 2

HOME AND SCHOOL

Introduction by Delwyn Tattum

Bullying is the concern of every school – it is in many respects the school's problem because it provides the location in which bullying can take place. Large numbers of children are brought together from a wide range of homes with a range of child-rearing practices. On a continuum of learning experiences they arrive from some homes that are violent and abusive, and at odds with much that the school and teachers value, cherish and seek to inculcate, whilst others come from homes in accord with the culture of the school and its sets of values, beliefs, habits and attitudes. Unfortunately, nothing in the home experiences of the latter group prepares them to cope with the overt aggression of some of their peers. For the potential bully the school is the place where she or he can practice and refine their skills of humiliation and intimidation.

In fact, schools are aggressive places, where bullying occurs much more frequently than teachers even think happen. Every piece of research demonstrates that teachers underestimate the amount of bullying when compared with the response of the pupils in the school. This is not surprising, as most bullying is secretive and carried out away from the eyes of adults. Most bullying occurs on the playground and the most frequented locale in the building is the toilets. Studies also show that bullying can take place in corridors and classrooms, under the eyes of teachers and others in authority. The journey to and from school provides unsupervised settings, especially when children have to be bussed.

In fact school provides many places and opportunities for bullies to pick out their victims, that is why every school, from nursery to large comprehensive, must have a carefully, worked-out policy which communicates the nature and unacceptability of bullying so that all persons associated with it are under no misapprehensions about how seriously the behaviour is viewed by the schools. Together with an overt reiteration of its policy every school needs to operationalise its value-position through a developed programme which covers all aspects of school life. This would be a whole-school response to bullying and in the Figure contained in this introduction to Part 2, 'From Crisis-management to Prevention', a range of strategies are presented. The diagram progresses from those which are reactive – in response to a problem after it occurs – to those which are more proactive approaches, in that they anticipate the critical times in a student's career when bullying is more likely to take place.

The chapters in this section offer a variety of proactive, preventative approaches, which is the general theme of the book. Moreover preventative approaches unequivocally declare that bullying is contrary to the ethos of the school and, when detected, will be severely dealt with. Finally, it is not suggested that these three responses are independent of each other but rather that they serve different purposes in a school's total approach to the problem. In fact crisis cases will be more effectively dealt with within a supportive, preventative ethos.

From Crisis-management to Prevention

Crisis-management Approaches	Intervention Strategies	Preventative Responses
Bully Courts No Blame Approach Shared concern Peer counselling Crisis care	Transition planning Peer support Playground supervision	Administration/Organisation Using the curriculum Community ethos

Reactive   **Proactive**

Crisis-management

In its anti-bullying programme, a school needs to have ways of supporting those who are bullied as well as methods of changing the attitudes and behaviour of the bullies. Recommended approaches include the use of sanctions, with expulsion from the school as the final action in demonstrating to pupils and parents that a school will not tolerate bullying. Other approaches include reasoning with bullies and trying to get them to appreciate how the victim feels. Some writers advocate the use of group pressure to influence the behaviour of bullies, as well as to encourage other students to take responsibility for their more vulnerable peers (see Chapter 7).

'Bully Courts' are a way of influencing a bully's behaviour through group pressure and other sanctions. Used in primary schools, the 'bench' may consist of two teachers and five elected children (Elliott, 1991). The next three Crisis-management approaches on the list, namely,'No Blame', 'Shared concern' and 'Peer counselling' are methods which require a teacher or student, as in the latter approach, to talk to persons involved in bullying in a non-threatening or non-accusative manner. The success of these approaches is heavily dependent on the teacher's or student's conciliatory and counselling skills in bringing the disputants to a resolution of the problem. (Maggie Robson deals with counselling in greater depth in Chapter 8.)

Finally, 'Crisis care' is a method which aims to formalise procedures and bring a degree of consistency to the way in which teachers handle bullying cases (Tattum and Tattum, 1996). For, when investigating cases, teachers ask each time the same six questions and get everyone involved to answer in writing.

- What happened?
- Why did it happen?
- Who was involved?
- Where did it take place?
- When did it take place?
- How do you think we can resolve this problem?

At the bottom of a pro forma containing the questions and filled-in answers, there should be a space for two signatures – the student's and that of the teacher conducting the interview, and the date. The pro forma should be used by all staff when dealing with cases of bullying. How the pro forma information should be subsequently used is described in detail, using a case study to illustrate the method, in Tattum and Tattum (1994).

Intervention strategies

These strategies recognise that there are critical times and places in which a child is particularly vulnerable. One such time is transition and in Chapter 4 we deal with from home to school transfer and in Tattum and Tattum (1992) there is an examination of school to school transfers and how secondary schools can liaise with their feeder primaries. One strategy is for primary schools to invite ex-pupils from the local secondary school to talk to their final year pupils about bullying.

'Peer support' can take many forms but in the context of transition the

'buddy' system has shown itself to be successful. Crucial factors are:
- Selection
- Training
- Allocation.

Not everyone is suited to being a buddy to a younger student and it is important that the position is seen as a privilege. In their training, students need to understand what their role entails and the purpose of the scheme. Finally, it is important to match each buddy with a new student who comes from the same primary school and locality. This creates an early association and in practical terms they will see each other as they travel to and from school, visit the same shops, and so on.

Many writers have pointed out the need for well-supervise playgrounds, where otherwise a great deal of bullying can take plac. Schools need to identify 'bullying hot-spots' and ensure that 'no-go' places do not exist, for example, toilets. But the most far-reachi changes to playground supervision would be to introduce a tra programme for midday supervisors and to make play area creative and constructive social and physical environments (T um and Herbert, 1993). Moreover, Blatchford (Tattum, 1993) broadens our perception of the affective curriculum as he points out that the playground is an important learning environment, for it is here that children learn the social and personal skills necessary for smooth and effective interaction with their peers.

Preventative responses

In Tattum (1993) a table of short-, medium- and long-term strategies is presented to develop the preventative responses that could be part of a whole-school approach to bullying. Initially, every school needs to review existing documents and procedures to see if they are adequate. Is bullying named in school prospectuses, year handbooks and the general discipline policy statement, and condemned as unacceptable behaviour? In the production of school statements, students should be closely involved in the process so that they identify with the school's aims.

Running concurrently with a school's awareness-raising efforts should be work to achieve shared understanding about what constitutes bullying behaviour. A staff training day should include a wide spectrum of supportive adults, such as governors, support and ancillary staff – most especially, midday supervisors. It is also advisable to carry out a survey to find out which children are involved in bullying according to age, sex, ability, etc, and where,

children] to get on with it. It's no good encouraging them to be too sensitive, they should learn to ignore it'.

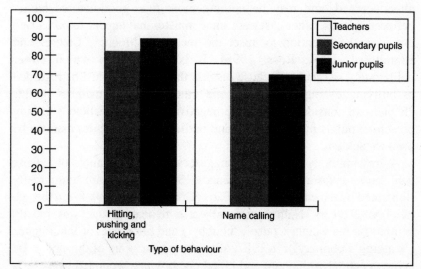

Fig : Percentage of teachers (N=138) and secondary (N=170) and juni .96) school pupils who regard hitting, kicking and pushing, and name- .alling, as bullying

Does it matter that many teachers and pupils do not regard teasing as bullying? We believe it does for a number of reasons. One of these relates to the likely links between attitudes and behaviour – it would not be unreasonable to suggest that how a pupil or teacher defines bullying is likely to impact to some extent on their actual behaviour. Thus, for example, a teacher who does view teasing as bullying may be more likely to intervene if she or he saw it take place, or respond more vigorously if it was reported to her or him, than another who does not view it as bullying. Such an attitude–behaviour link has been suggested for other types of pupil misbehaviour (Chazan, Laing and Harper, 1987) but it has not been discussed or researched widely in relation to bullying per se. Similarly, within a school context and elsewhere, it is important that all pupils realise that bullying can take many different forms, and moreover, that all of these different manifestations, including teasing, are unacceptable. If this was not the case, it is unlikely that steps to reduce the problem of bullying will be optimally successful.

What are the effects of verbal bullying?

Another important reason why we are disturbed by our finding that many teachers and pupils do not regard teasing as bullying, stems from the possible negative effects of some types of teasing. A number of writers have noted that while many instances of teasing are enjoyed by all concerned, and may be nothing more than good-natured banter between friends, other cases are more sinister and appear to be carried out with the intention to upset the recipient (Mooney, Creeser and Blatchford, 1991; Ross, 1996). It is those cases which either deliberately or otherwise cause distress that we think must be regarded as bullying by pupils, teachers and others. In the remainder of this chapter, we consider the possible negative effects of malicious teasing on school pupils in more detail, and outline some strategies that can be used to tackle it.

A growing body of evidence suggests that some instances of teasing can have devastating consequences. Such effects are graphically illustrated by the case of Nathan Faris (Greenbaum, 1989). From the age of about 9 years, Nathan was subjected to teasing that was mostly centred on his weight ('fatso', 'chubby') and high level of intelligence ('walking dictionary'). In 1987, after about four years of this abuse, he came to school with a gun and killed one boy and wounded two others before killing himself. It came to light after the incident that most of the pupils who had teased him, or who witnessed its occurrence, did not think that it was particularly severe. It did not appear that either the teachers or the other pupils regarded the teasing as bullying, and this is a likely reason why nothing was done to stop it happening. Nevertheless, as Ross (1996) recently pointed out, it is the subjectivity of the pain caused by teasing that is important. She stated that, 'Others' opinion of the teasing is completely irrelevant because their judgements have no relation to how the victim feels. Children's appraisals *must* be accepted at face value: If they say it is terrible, then it is terrible. This is an extremely important point that cannot be overemphasized'.

Even in the absence of such extreme effects, many children appear to be so incensed by malicious teasing that they retaliate with aggression and the interaction escalates into all-out fighting (Boulton, 1993a and b; Mooney, Creeser and Blatchford, 1991).

Along with a colleague, Aber Arazi, we are carrying out a study to examine what adults can remember about the hurtful effects of teasing, and what they felt now about their being teased as children. Of the 137 adults we have contacted so far, 94 (68.6 per cent) indicated that they had been teased at school. Seventy-two per cent of these said they remembered feeling sad at the time the teasing took place, and 33 per cent said they felt sad now about these experiences. Similarly, 58 per cent indicated that they remembered feeling depressed as children because they were teased, and 11 per cent indicated that they currently

pressed when they thought about this childhood teasing. Our
s only intended to be a preliminary investigation of the possible
l effects of childhood teasing – it suffers from all of the
limitations associated with retrospective, self-report methods of data
collection, notably the possibility of biased and incomplete
recollections and reports. Nevertheless, along with the other evidence
we have from studies with pupils, the data we have collected so far
support the suggestion that teasing often can have harmful effects, and
these may last much longer than the episodes of teasing themselves.

Why verbal bullying may be overlooked

Given this conclusion, it would seem difficult to reconcile the fact that,
on the one hand, many adults can vividly recall the distress that they felt
when they were teased at school with our finding that so many teachers
do not regard teasing as bullying, espouse a 'sticks and stones approach'
and think that pupils should cope with it on their own. One possibility
is that in our study, it was those teachers who had not been teased as
children, or who had not been distressed when they had been teased,
who did not regard teasing as bullying.

Another possibility is that teachers *can* appreciate the distress that
teasing may cause but do not have the time they would like to attend to
all instances of misbehaviour. They may feel that they have to prioritise
the attention that they give to different types of pupil misbehaviour. This
is reflected in the comment of one junior school teacher we spoke to
who said, 'I've been a teacher for more than twenty years, and I would
say that the children are definitely getting more unruly. It seems to me
that after almost every break time there is someone saying, "Miss,
Johnny hit me", or "Karen is being nasty to me". I try to take all of them
seriously but I just have to let some of them go otherwise I'd have to
leave the rest of the class while I sorted them out. I often find myself
saying to children who say they have been called names, "Just ignore
them and they will soon find something better to do". "I don't like doing
this but feel I have to." This is not an isolated view. In a recent survey,
it was found that teachers at one in five of primary schools, and one in
four of secondary schools, indicated that pupils were more aggressive at
break times now than they were five years ago, and that it was
becoming more difficult to deal with misbehaviour (Blatchford and
Sumpner, 1996).

A third reason that might explain why many teachers (and pupils
themselves) do not regard teasing as bullying stems from the nature of
teasing. Pawluk (1989) argued that teasing is characterised by

ambiguity because it contains both irritating and light-hearted qualities and because it often contains hidden messages and implications. Moreover, what one child might find upsetting, another might find playful, and what one child might find upsetting on one occasion they might find playful on another occasion (see the case of Nathan Faris, described above). This means that it may be difficult for recipients and adult onlookers to determine the intention of the teaser, and for the teaser to know the effect of her or his actions. Nevertheless, Pawluk argued that ambiguity in teasing can be overemphasised. She reported that it is often the case that the intention or meaning is quickly realised.

To our minds, there are striking parallels here between verbal and physical interactions. Just as it is the case with teasing, interactions that involve hitting, kicking, wrestling and other bodily contacts fall along a play/aggression continuum. At one end is playful fighting which participants greatly enjoy and choose to engage in frequently. At the other end is true aggression/fighting which participants do not seem to enjoy. Many adults, including those who work with children, often make mistakes distinguishing between the two (Boulton, 1993c, 1996). Nevertheless, no adult would conclude that just because some fighting can be playful in nature, and because it may be difficult to distinguish between playful and aggressive fighting, that all fighting should be allowed to happen. It would be somewhat puzzling, therefore, if teachers and other adults used this line of reasoning to support their decision to allow children to tease one another.

Whatever the reason for the laissez-faire attitude towards teasing among many teachers (and pupils), it is now clear that such a view should be challenged. We want to reinforce the point that pupils should be discouraged from teasing one another if the intention is to cause distress, or there is the least suspicion that this is the effect, just as much as they should be discouraged from hitting and kicking one another.

How to tackle verbal bullying

What steps can be taken to combat the problem of malicious teasing? In our view, teasing is bullying just as much as is physical assault, and so the optimum approach would be to widen people's views of bullying to include this type of social interaction. Once this has been achieved, then almost all of a school's attempts to stop physical bullying would also serve to discourage pupils from teasing one another in a way that causes distress. This means that interventions at the level of individual pupils, at the level of classes, and right up to the level of whole-school policy which involves the wider community are just as appropriate for teasing as they are for physical forms of bullying.

Despite this claim that it would be useful if schools did not distinguish between teasing and physical forms of bullying, and tackled them with the same approaches, the verbal nature of teasing means that some types of anti-bullying work may be especially useful in helping pupils deal with verbal as opposed to physical bullying. We shall consider some of these here.

There are many possibilities for working with individual pupils, and at least four programmes have been developed to equip pupils with the skills needed to dissuade peers from verbally bullying them (Ross, 1996; Kellerman, 1981; Phillips, 1989; and M. J. Smith, 1986). As Ross (1996) recently pointed out, these programmes incorporate some or all of the following principles:

(i) *Nonreward* teaches victims to avoid reacting in a way that would encourage further verbal attacks

(ii) *Verbal punishment* calls for verbal retaliations that discourage further verbal attacks

(iii) *Assertiveness training* sets out to change the submissive demeanour or behaviour of victims in such a way as to make further teasing less likely

(iv) *Understanding the teaser's motives* encourages victims to appreciate that it is the teaser and not themselves who are to blame for the teasing and to use this knowledge to choose the most effective response to discourage further verbal harassment.

Space constraints prevent a detailed discussion of each of these major programmes, and the interested reader is strongly advised to consult the original texts. All of these texts are presented in a way that practitioners will find useful. Nevertheless, we shall consider the strengths and weaknesses of some of the major components of these anti-teasing initiatives that are aimed at individual pupils.

The principle of nonreward is the core of Kellerman's programme. It is based firmly on the behaviourist notion of extinction which states that behaviour will reduce in frequency if it is not followed by consequences that the individual finds rewarding. Translated into children's interactions, this means that victims are encouraged to ignore any teasing that they should experience. Kellerman showed that this type of response may succeed for some children some of the time, and as such nonreward is something that teachers and other adults concerned with helping victims may want to consider. There are, however, a number of important caveats. One is that this approach might inadvertently give children the impression that adults' responses to their complaints of teasing are limited to 'just ignore it and it will go away'. In our view, it would be more desirable if steps could be taken to ensure that victims actually have the capacity to ignore the teasing. After all, many pupils who tease their peers try to pick a topic that they know will provoke a reaction from their victims. Often they refer not to the victims themselves but to family members, and many children find it hard to show no reaction in these cases (Boulton, 1993a and b; Mooney, Creeser and Blatchford, 1991). (How would *you* feel if a disparaging comment about your mother/father/wife/husband/partner/best friend was used to provoke an angry reaction?)

Even supposing victims were able to control the anger they felt when they were teased, asking them to show no reaction is contrary to the norm of reciprocity which appears to be a feature of junior and secondary school pupils' peer groups (Boulton, 1993a and b; Mooney, Creeser and Blatchford, 1991). Support for the existence of this norm comes from the robust finding that most pupils report feeling compelled to retaliate to undesirable behaviour because they believe that if they did not 'pay the other person back', they would get a reputation for being weak and so be even more likely to be picked on in the future. Parents may contribute to the development of this norm – many endorse the tenet of 'you must fight back' and deliberately try to instil it in their children (Miller and Sperry, 1987). Kochenderfer and Ladd (personal communication) have some preliminary evidence that fighting back may actually make bullying worse.

All in all then, it may be difficult for many pupils to refrain from responding to teasing. This was recognised by Phillips, who built into her programme the need to look closely at children's capacities to do so. She suggested that teaching individuals how to give an 'emotional shrug' may help those who find it difficult to remain silent during episodes of teasing. This involves adopting a stance that gives the impression of 'I'm not bothered by what you say'. In order to help children keep calm while the teasing takes place, and so give an emotional shrug, Phillips suggested that they could be encouraged to think about a great moment in their lives, some event of which they are particularly proud. They can then be encouraged to think about this when they are teased, thus making it less likely that they will give out a weak rejoinder that would only serve to reinforce the teaser. Phillips' programme also allows victims to say *something* during the teasing but only to agree if the teaser said something that was true (e.g. 'That's right, I can't run very fast'). It is thought that this serves the dual purpose of easing the tension that might nevertheless build up in the victims by letting them say something, and at the same time reducing the impact of the teasing. Phillips noted that role play may help the victim consolidate some of the strategies that her programme tries to teach victims of teasing.

A different approach to combating teasing is taken in the Social Thinking and Reasoning (STAR) Programme developed by M. J. Smith (1986). Here the emphasis is on equipping victims with skills and strategies for knowing what to say when they are faced with teasing and other types of conflict situations. Rather than remaining passive and saying nothing, Smith advocates encouraging victims to play an active role in discouraging teasers. He claimed that a range of verbal strategies are likely to be of use to most children, once they have been mastered. In *fogging*, victims respond with a neutral statement that attempts to de-escalate the situation ('You might think that', 'Maybe'). In *mirroring*, victims simply repeat back what has been said ('So you think I'm a weirdo?'). The *broken record technique* involves saying the same thing over and over again (Teaser: Run across the playground so we can all see how slow you are. Victim: Not now, I'm playing a game. Teaser: Go on, give us all a laugh. Victim: Not now, I'm playing a game. Teaser: What's wrong, can't you even run across the playground? Victim: Not now, I'm playing a game. Teaser: Are you going to run or not? Victim: Not now, I'm playing a game. Teaser: This is boring.) The idea behind all of these techniques (and others that Smith advocates) is to make the tormentor bored and so want to withdraw from the situation because they are not able to provoke a reaction that shows that the victim is upset or angry.

To many adults, the techniques employed in the STAR programme may appear simple enough. Nevertheless, in evaluating it, Ross (1996) recently noted that it calls for a lot of hard work and practice on the part of the child and the adult helper. Pupils who are teased must be given many opportunities to practice the techniques in 'safe' situations before trying them out for real. We are in agreement with Ross, that if children are able to master these techniques for being assertive, then they are likely to enjoy both immediate and long-term benefits.

To help reinforce the point that it is appropriate to use similar interventions to tackle both bullying in general and teasing in particular (see above), it is worth noting that the STAR programme has a very similar content to the Assertiveness Training programme for bullied pupils devised by Sharp, Cowie and Smith (1994). In both cases the general aim is to equip victims with the verbal and social skills that they can use to defuse harassment when it actually takes place, and to make the bully less likely to find the situation rewarding.

It is also appropriate to use anti-teasing interventions that operate at the level of the class. Once again, we believe they should not be separated from interventions aimed at tackling bullying. Where appropriate, the aim of whole-class interventions could be to widen pupils' conceptions of bullying to include things like malicious teasing. The rationale for this approach, as noted above, is that some pupils may be less likely to behave in a certain way if they view this as bullying, or they might be more prepared to help a child that someone else is harassing in this way. The anti-bullying literature contains several guidelines that may help in this respect (Boulton and Flemington, 1996; Cowie and Sharp, 1994; Gobey, 1991; see also Chapters 6, 7 and 9 of this volume). Cowie and Sharp looked at the use of children's literature as a means of introducing the topic of bullying and how pupils conceive it. In particular, they examined the impact of *The Heartstone Odyssey* by Arvan Kumar (1988). The book demonstrates the unfairness of bullying, especially racial harassment, and introduces anti-bullying strategies. In this study, junior school pupils listened as the teacher read out the story, and discussed it in debriefing sessions. The pupils were then asked what they had learned from the book. Common responses (not quantified by Cowie and Sharp) were along the lines of 'Don't bully' in general, as well as 'Don't call names' in particular (see Chapter 12).

In a similar way, Gobey reported that drama and role play can extend and deepen secondary school pupils' conceptions of bullying. Again, more pupils (not quantified by Gobey) were found to regard teasing as bullying following this type of intervention.

We have also found that anti-bullying videos can help in this respect (Boulton and Flemington, 1996). An experimental design was adopted so that it was possible to state how many pupils changed their minds about viewing teasing as bullying, as a consequence of watching the video. Participants were shown a list of eight behaviours and asked to indicate which ones they did, and which they did not, see as bullying. They were asked to do this on two occasions separated by two weeks. The analysis focused on those pupils who did change their minds over the duration of the project. More than half (53.3 per cent) of those pupils who watched Central Television's Sticks and Stones anti-bullying video changed to include teasing in their definition of bullying, whereas less than a quarter (22.9 per cent) of those who did not see the video changed in this direction. This difference was statistically significant.

Anti-bullying work at the level of the whole school/community is also relevant. One widely used initiative at this level is the whole-school anti-bullying policy. Sharp and Thompson (1994) noted that policy development can be made effective if it proceeds via five distinct stages

– awareness raising, consultation, preparation of draft and transition to final policy, communication and implementation, and maintenance and review. We would like to suggest that the first stage is particularly useful to help ensure that all members of the school community regard malicious teasing as bullying. According to Sharp and Thompson, awareness-raising should provide people with up-to-date information about the nature and extent of bullying so that they are in a position to make informed decisions about it, help dispel some of the myths that surround bullying, and facilitate a consensus about what bullying is. We hope that some of the data and arguments presented in this chapter will serve to provide readers with up-to-date information about malicious teasing, and so help them accept that it is bullying, if they don't already.

Conclusion

In conclusion, the ambiguous nature of teasing presents teachers and others concerned with children's well-being with a problem. On the one hand, teasing may be playful and enjoyed by all parties. On the other hand, pupils often use teasing to harass their peers, and many instances of teasing cause distress that may be long-lasting and severe. Data we have collected and reported here suggests that work needs to be done to convince more pupils and teachers that the difference between the two general types of teasing is important, and that whereas the former is acceptable, the latter is bullying. As such, it should be made clear to all members of a school community that malicious teasing should not, and will not, be tolerated. This chapter has outlined a number of interventions that may help achieve this worthy goal.

Chapter 6

Using group dynamics to support vulnerable children: including victims of school bullying

Kay Fitzherbert and Sue Yeo

Introduction

Kay Fitzherbert, Director, National Pyramid Trust

Why do some otherwise ordinary children develop into habitual bullies, and others into victims? Genetic predisposition may be part of the answer, but I doubt that an infant can be destined from birth to become, irrevocably, the one or the other. Becoming a full-blown bully or victim takes years of practice; you can't build a career overnight and something may even prevent you from ever getting to the top!

I first became seriously interested in prevention in the early 1970s when I was the social worker on a home/school liaison project in the London Borough of Ealing. All my referrals came from the high school in my patch and concerned children already in such deep trouble that my contribution to their plight was rarely more than a 'mopping up' operation. As far as their education was concerned, these youngsters had already reached the end of the line – and they were usually no more than about 14 years of age.

It therefore came as something of a shock to discover that their primary teachers often remembered these same young troublemakers with affection, as charming children with quite a lot to offer. Yes, they had possibly been emotionally disturbed, neglected and under-functioning, but when they knew them, they could still be contained. Interfering in their home situation or referring them to an outside agency would have been wrong, equivalent to rejecting a child who had done no wrong and was more sinned against than sinning.

My colleagues and I wanted to find out how these primary schools saw their role in relation to pupils whose failures at school were evidently linked to pressure in other areas of their lives: pressures that were pushing them inexorably down the path of giving up, failing, becoming alienated and, finally, being excluded from the mainstream. We conducted a borough-wide survey to find out about their procedures for dealing with such children.

The result left us puzzled for we could discern no single policy or practice. As many procedures were in use as there were schools, ranging from the most caring involvement in individual children's welfare to doing nothing and not even understanding the gist of our questions. We concluded that preventive intervention, picking up and responding to early warning signs of future failure, wasn't on the official education agenda.

With the plight of my 14-year-old problem children in mind, I had by now become convinced that primary, not secondary school, was the logical place for social work input, and that the focus should not be picking up the pieces of disaster, but prevention. It was the ideal context for identifying children who were starting to give up and for mobilising support that might succeed in keeping them in the mainstream of school – and life. Incipient bullies – and their victims – were just the kind of children who, I was sure, could still be diverted into less damaging careers if they were caught in time.

In 1978, I was awarded a grant by the then Social Science Research Council to do a piece of action research called 'Developing an Integrated Preventive Child Care System focused on the Primary School' (Fitzherbert, 1991). The idea was to test some simple procedures that could become the basis of an easily replicable preventive system, for use by any school. It would combine teachers identifying vulnerable children and bringing in other professionals with responsibilities for children in the community, who were normally only called on when there was a crisis. Everyone would get together to plan appropriate preventive intervention for each child identified as at risk. This new way of working together was to be achieved within existing resources on the principle that an investment of everyone's time in prevention would inevitably pay off through the reduction in crisis work later on.

I conducted my experiment in the London Borough of Hounslow from 1978–82, based in three schools, involving dozens of teachers, support workers from other agencies and following experimental ('E') children and a smaller control group ('C') through three years of schooling. By the end of the project, several years of trial and error had produced the Pyramid System, a simple and effective preventive structure that could be operated by any primary school. A follow-up study three years later found that four-fifths of the 'E' children, identified in primary school as at risk of not coping in secondary, were surviving normally in the mainstream. Three-quarters of the 'C' group, identified in the same way, but given no special treatment, were by now in special units or had dropped out of school altogether.

On the strength of these findings, Hounslow Education Department in 1984 took over the scheme – known as the 'Muppet Club Project' – as an additional support service for its neediest schools. I became its organiser, but eventually left to make it more widely known. The Department of Health and the Norman Trust provided funding for two projects in Hillingdon and Bristol to test if the methods developed in Hounslow under research conditions could be effective in other areas. In 1994 the BBC Children in Need Appeal enabled a further project to start up in South Glamorgan (now Cardiff County and the Vale of Glamorgan).

Putting the Pyramid System into practice

Sue Yeo, Project Manager, National Pyramid Trust

> To help all children achieve self esteem, cope with school and succeed in life. (National Pyramid Trust)

The National Pyramid Trust was established by Kay Fitzherbert in December 1992 as an independent registered charity to offer an effective method of preventive work with primary age children. The Trust believes that by reaching vulnerable children as early as seven, developing problems whether social, emotional or behavioural can often be 'nipped in the bud'.

In October 1994, I was appointed as Project Co-ordinator for a three-year pilot project in South Glamorgan (now Cardiff County and the Vale of Glamorgan). My brief was to put the Pyramid System into operation in local primary schools using a multi-agency approach. This chapter will highlight the work that has been undertaken, explaining each procedure in action and the response so far to our work in Wales. In our first year of operation, six schools were involved and 12 in our second year, all in areas of high social need. The project is now based at University of Wales Institute, Cardiff (UWIC).

The procedures

The system developed by the Trust consists of three simple managed procedures:

(1) screening;
(2) multi-agency consultation focused on individual children;
(3) short-term activity clubs to promote good mental health in vulnerable children.

Information packs and guidance are provided for every school.

1. Screening – a trigger to action

'Its completion certainly raised staff awareness of the specific needs of our children as a result of its fine focus.' (Deputy Headteacher)

Class teachers screen the all round development of a whole year group of children, usually seven- and eight-year-olds, using a simple checklist provided by the Trust to look at their educational progress as well as their physical, social and emotional well-being. It is not intended to record achievement or ability but to help teachers organise their thoughts as the first step towards initiating action. Across the year group class teachers identify children who cause them no concern, some concern and a lot of concern. During the second part of the process, the multi-agency consultation, this latter group will be discussed. When repeated annually, this screening procedure provides a preventive safety net for all the children passing through the school.

Feedback on the screening process from the schools is that it is easy to use. The Trust emphasises the importance of every child being considered using this systematic approach as children may be overlooked who cause no bother but are sad or isolated in class or the playground. Teachers have often said after the screening exercise that they might have overlooked 'him' or 'her.'

'The checklist was a useful tool for focusing in on all the children.' (Class teacher)

'It highlighted the large numbers of children who give cause for concern in various ways.' (Class teacher)

2. Multi-agency consultation

'The meetings were arguably the most valuable part. Apart from giving us leverage with external support agencies, they provided the school with a focus, a prime opportunity to share information about a whole year group.' (Head teacher)

This second procedure of holding Inter-Disciplinary (I.D.) meetings is recognised by schools as being extremely valuable. Representatives from school support services (school nurse, pupil support, education welfare, social services) are sent a list of the school year group, highlighting children to be discussed and are invited to two Inter-Disciplinary meetings.

At the first, class teachers present their concerns about the children they have identified through the screening process. The aim is to decide upon at least one positive strategy per child. Follow-up action may then have to be taken by the school or other agencies present. For eight to ten children, attendance at a Pyramid Club will be recommended.

Natalie's class teacher was aware that her writing was very small but until the Inter-Disciplinary meeting was unaware that she had a serious sight problem which had been raised by the school nurse. As a result, Natalie was moved nearer to the blackboard and because of her quietness was given a Pyramid Club place.

Andrew experienced ongoing difficulties with attendance, care and management at home. The family were known to the Education Welfare Officer and social services. A cross-referral was made at the Inter-Disciplinary meeting for social services to follow this up.

Charleen had been displaying odd behaviour at times and was often withdrawn. There was also a growing concern about hygiene. She had no intercommunication with other children. It was decided to give her a Pyramid Club place and also to refer her to the school's Care Committee where children causing the greatest concern are reviewed.

The second Inter-Disciplinary meeting is attended by the same representatives plus the Pyramid Club Leaders for that school. Feedback is given on any progress the children previously discussed have made. The Club Leaders also give an account of their observations of the children they have worked with and class teachers comment on any perceived changes in those children.

Year group sizes have varied from 21 children through to 86 and, on average, a third of the children in any one year are discussed. In one school with 80 children in the year group, 43 were discussed at the I.D. meeting. This showed a great deal of commitment to the process as each meeting took the best part of a morning or afternoon. The feedback from this school has been extremely positive, with the head teacher stating that for the relatively small amount of time invested, the meetings were the most effective method of getting to know the children.

'The Inter-Disciplinary meetings were the most valuable aspects of the project from my point of view. We very rarely meet these people (support agencies) except in a crisis situation. It is possible that links were forged that will aid communication in the future and thus help all the children.' (Head teacher)

'The meetings were valuable in that they not only focused attention on children who could join the club but also on other children who had specific needs.' (Deputy Headteacher)

3. Short-term activity clubs

'Over time the children seemed more relaxed. They talked more and relationships improved. By the end, they liked doing things together, whatever they were doing.' (Volunteer Club Leader)

At the first Inter-Disciplinary meetings, 8 or 10 children are selected for an after school Pyramid Club which is run according to a proven formula by trained volunteers from UWIC. The clubs run over a ten week period with nine weekly after school sessions run for one-and-a-half hours and a day trip or outing is also included. There are three leaders per club. The clubs help to boost the confidence, personal resilience and social skills of vulnerable children. Their value is supported by the research of Professor Kolvin (1981) who found play groups the most effective technique for promoting mental health in his extensive study carried out in Newcastle in the 1970s.

The children

Many children in need of attention and having trouble in school will make themselves known to teachers fairly quickly. However, there are less visible children who do not have obvious problems and troubles but their teachers know they are not thriving and they give them cause for concern. It is these 'invisible children' that the Pyramid process is so good at highlighting so that preventive input can be given to them now, rather than waiting for problems to develop later on.

Who are these children? They are often shy, withdrawn, less socially skilled than their peers, victims of bullying, potential bullies, from sheltered backgrounds or are young carers. They may appear sad and often be on their own in the playground or on the periphery of groups. Through their eccentric behaviour, they may be isolating themselves. Every school I visit can identify children like this and after doing the screening often come up with other children they had not thought of before.

'Sad little case', 'weight of the world on his shoulders', 'poor little dab', 'living in the shadow of his sister', 'life is lived on the brink of tears', 'invisible man' are just some of the comments made at the Inter-Disciplinary meetings. It is these children that the Pyramid Clubs are particularly good at helping.

The Pyramid process works with seven- to nine-year-olds. Research has shown that at this stage in their development, children crave positive peer group relationships. Mortimer Schiffer (1976) refers to children's 'social hunger' for groups and socialisation at this age. Pyramid identifies those who are unable to form positive peer group relationships for themselves and with the help and support of trained Leaders, enables them to build such relationships in a small, secure group where new behaviours can be tried and tested. The confidence built up over the sessions often spills over into the classroom and acts as a catalyst for future development.

Activity groups are the ideal answer for children who have problems with personal and social relationships, who lack confidence and motivation, are immature, anxious or unhappy, or are living under particular pressures at home. A group experience can often stimulate that extra bit of optimism and perseverance needed to survive such pressures. As the group develops, children learn to co-operate with one another, helping one another and realising their own and others' strengths and weaknesses. A sense of ownership develops and whether a child presents initially as a victim or bully, peer group pressure comes into play to encourage or thwart an individual child's behaviour. A group dynamic evolves, helping children to work or play co-operatively, removing any stigma for slow learners. Friendships are made, and relationships are built up helping the socially isolated children, those who are seen as 'victims' or painfully shy and the more out-acting children. Social learning is positively reinforced in a group context where children learn to share, co-operate and take risks in a secure environment.

'The Invisible Man' was the description given of Michael at the first I.D. meeting. He was 'painfully introverted and tensed up – not just shy'. Club Leaders were concerned about him at first, and his body language. He would avoid eye contact and even cover his head. Then on Week 6 of club they did face painting and Michael was 'unbelievable'. He had become that tiger. He even offered to start circle time and has since rolled around laughing. His teacher has seen a definite change in class where he will now put his hand up and offer to go out the front, which he would never have done before.

In 1995 a researcher from Surrey University conducted an evaluation of 13 clubs run by the Trust that year. He found that of those children who attended a club, 59.6 per cent showed improvement in self-esteem according to the teachers, with 24.3 per cent of non-attendees not showing any improvement. Also the results indicate there was an improvement in writing, showing that with increased self-confidence, the children were able to express themselves better.

'His confidence has improved. His work has come on in leaps and bounds and he will now have a go at working on his own.' (Class teacher)

Some 'invisible children' who are victimised feel helpless and isolated and suppress their anger, only to erupt later on as school bullies. Through the positive intervention that Pyramid Clubs provide this can be prevented.

Club leaders

'... belonging to an organised peer-group of play mates can enhance the social and emotional development of young children, provided the group leaders know what they are about.' (Foreword by Professor Frederick H. Stone in *Children Need Groups*, Silveira 1988)

Each club made up of 8 or 10 children has three Club Leaders. This allows for a good child to adult ratio and flexibility in addressing individual needs. During the first year of the project when six clubs ran, half my volunteers came from the primary education course at UWIC and others from social care courses, qualified teachers and University College. Through the interest of the Countering Bullying Unit based at UWIC in our work, the Welsh Pyramid Project itself has relocated to the Institute, which has certainly helped the project to develop. In our second year when 14 clubs were requested by 12 schools, all 42 volunteers came from UWIC.

All Club Leaders take part in four training sessions where they are introduced to the work of the Trust and have experiential input on working with groups, running clubs and team building. Other important issues such as child protection, the needs of the child, practical activities, sharing responsibility and confidentiality are also covered. Along with the training, the leaders are given a Club Handbook and Information Pack which mirror the training input and Pyramid Ethos (Fitzherbert and Ford, 1993).

In her book, Mia Kellmer Pringle (1980) identified four essential ingredients children need to experience if they are to grow and mature into healthy adults. These are:

- Love and security
- Praise and recognition
- New experiences
- Responsibility

The Pyramid training emphasises these ingredients as important components of club life and volunteers discuss and practise ways of mirroring them. A suggested framework is given for club sessions allowing for individual flexibility. Feedback on the training suggests that we have pitched it at the right level. The commitment of project volunteers remains extremely high. Their creative and imaginative use of club time is very impressive and feedback from the schools is full of praise for their input.

The Clubs

'Club's wicked!' (Craig, a member of 'The Smart Lot Club')

So what does go on in club? The loose framework for any club session is that of a beginning, middle and an end and within that lots of different things take place. The whole ethos is about participation and co-operation rather than competition and with a ratio of three adults to 8 to 10 children, this can be achieved. Children are given the opportunity to belong to *their* group! One of the first things they do is choose the Club name, *The Friendly Balloon Club*, *The Wizzity Club*, *The Funky Fun Club* and *The Monster Club* to name but a few.

It is important that boundaries are set of what is and is not acceptable behaviour in club, which adds to the security. This is where the skills of the volunteers come into play as they discuss with the children the rules for their club. They ask the children to think of rules that will help club be a fun place to be. Often children come up with 'no, this ...', 'no, that ...' and rephrase them in a more positive light. Volunteers find that the children come up with basic rules about politeness and safety and generally respecting each other. *'Be nice to one another'*, *'Help everyone to have fun'*, *'Listen to each other'*. The children stick to the rules and often remind the leaders about them! Everyone is a club member.

Over the ten week period, the Club Leaders aim to develop group cohesion and a sense of belonging. Once the name and rules have been sorted some clubs design badges or special I.D. cards with photos and personal information included. Sessions will include co-operative play, cooking or preparing a snack, arts and craft activities and Circle Time. The children may work in pairs, small groups or all together. Whatever takes place, everyone is included. Those who do not want to take part can sit out, but they are always told that there is a place for them and nine times out of ten they will join in with the rest once the activity begins.

Half way through the life of a club, an outing or trip takes place and this is often recognised by the volunteers as the time when club members jell. It can also be the time when some members find their voices. One thing that strikes all the volunteers is how well behaved the children are.

Victoria was painfully quiet and shy. After her club trip, her mother rang one of the Club Leaders to thank them as since getting home, Victoria hadn't stopped talking about where they went and what they did.

Feedback

'The effect is dramatic in some cases and beneficial in all. It's hard to really grasp why something so simple is so significant.' (Head teacher)

Quiet, lonely children are often seen 'coming out of their shells' through their club experiences. Over-protected children may take on the role of 'baby' at club initially and often thrive and 'become a bit of a leader' towards the end of club as Jamie did. He tried many things out for the first time. Other children may display no spark in school, yet shine in club.

Rebecca was described as 'on cloud 9' at the first I.D. meeting, day-dreaming most of the time. Her teacher noticed a dramatic change in her. 'She's not at all like that in class now. She's awake, alert and a lot happier in school.' She comes up and hugs the teacher which she never did before.

Whatever else may be going on in these children's lives, Pyramid Clubs give them an opportunity to feel safe, relax and have a good time within a small group. For many, this opportunity acts as a catalyst and marked changes are noticed. For others, any change or development may be noticed well after club has ended.

Emma started school in the middle of a term, without any friendships and was very quiet. She enjoyed club and apart from the club outing remained very quiet. After the summer holidays, Emma returned to school a 'changed girl'. She was mixing and making new friendships and moving around groups in her class. Her class teacher was convinced that her Pyramid Club experiences had helped her to open out.

Some teachers' comments

'A very positive intervention.' (Head teacher)

'Those children who were sad and withdrawn or had a poor self-image gained from the extra attention and encouragement and also from the sense of being 'chosen', of being the 'special ones'. For one or two there has also been the knock-on effect of Mum finding a replacement activity such as swimming club when the club ended.' (Head teacher)

'Extraordinary change in her. Really, really come out of herself.' (Class teacher)

Comments from parents

'Chris enjoyed himself so much that he keeps talking about going again. I think as his parent it was one of the best things he ever participated in. Thank you for letting him take part in your wonderful project.'

'I believe there should be a club such as yours available to all children after school. Julie has benefited enormously from the quality time you were able to provide.'

And the children

'I learnt to be friends with other children and share stuff and make stuff for them.'

'I enjoyed club because it was something for me to do after school and it stopped me from being bored. Every week we had something different to do so all the other days you were looking forwards and trying to guess what we would do and I thought it was really good.'

'You'll have a fun time and once you get to know the club leaders it gets funner and funner.'

'I learnt that you've got to be kind to one another.'

Conclusion

Since coming to Wales, the Trust has helped teachers to screen 889 children. Of these, 318 were discussed at Inter-Disciplinary meetings and at least one positive strategy was identified for each child. A total of 179 children have taken up the opportunity of being part of a Pyramid Club. Research has shown that children with low self-esteem and who are socially withdrawn are more likely to be bullied and be the 'victims' at school. Pyramid Clubs give these children an opportunity to thrive, gain in confidence and personal resilience so they are no longer targets. From a secure base their positive peer group experience enables them to take risks and develop friendships and relationships. They are no longer isolated. Children who exhibit bullying behaviour come to see other children as having strengths and weaknesses like themselves, and experience the power of the group through peer group pressure. And it works! Some children blossom purely by being chosen for club. That in itself is enough to give them the boost they need. Many enjoy the opportunity of having quality adult attention over the ten weeks. Others find their voice for the first time. A few of the children change dramatically over the club period, others make changes in some areas and there are those concerning whom very little change is noticed. But what our research has found is that not only are positive changes maintained but, over time, further positive effects are noticed. Those children who at first appear not to have benefited much can make significant progress later on.

The simplicity of the Pyramid model makes it very accessible and the Trust's vision is of every primary school in the land one day incorporating Pyramid as a preventive mechanism. The model is flexible and can easily be used. There is increasing concern about disaffected children and the Pyramid Trust offers support at a crucial time in their development, which can prevent problems arising. Working together with schools and support services, we can help these children to cope with school and succeed in life.

Note

For more information, write or telephone to: The National Pyramid Trust, 204 Church Road, Hanwell, London, W7 3BP. Tel: (0181) 579 5108

Chapter 7

Using conflict resolution and peer mediation to tackle bullying

Hilary Stacey, Pat Robinson and Daniel Cremin

Introduction

There is a growing awareness that tackling bullying needs to be done in an holistic way, not just by dealing with the symptoms as they occur. Bullying is not just a problem for the 27 per cent of victims in primary schools and the 10 per cent of victims in secondary schools who admit to being victims (DFE, 1994a), it is a problem that is manifest throughout the whole community of which the school is a part. Witnesses to bullying, the families of children who attend the school and members of the wider community are all involved. Approaches that focus on bullies and victims and that rely on extra policing by teachers and other adults are exacerbating the problem. It is harmful to label bullies and victims, and to imply that bullying can only be stopped by vigilant adults.

By using a social psychological approach, we are suggesting that schools can work with all children to create a community that is intolerant of bullying. The Sheffield bullying research project funded by the DFE found that 80 per cent of children dislike bullying, but that many of them did not know how to stop it. By raising children's awareness of their rights, and by supporting them to access their rights, we have been able to develop an approach which empowers both primary and secondary pupils to reduce bullying on behalf of themselves and each other. Our approach is centred around using a variety of teaching methods, including a device called Circle Time, to teach pupils conflict resolution, peer mediation skills and what Nancy Eisenberg (Eisenberg and Mussen, 1989) has called pro-social skills, as part of the curriculum.

Mediation is a structured process in which a neutral third party assists *voluntary* participants to resolve their dispute. It is being used increasingly in a variety of contexts, to resolve conflicts in schools, in neighbourhoods, in families and most recently as a Government recommended part of divorce proceedings.

Mediation is not about deciding who is right or wrong, or apportioning blame, or even focusing on the past any more than is necessary to help the disputants to work out the way forward, nor is it about the mediator offering advice and solutions. The whole process attempts to find mutually acceptable long-term solutions devised by the disputants themselves and takes place in a safe and structured environment, in which the mediator is in control of the process. It is not a panacea and can only exist as part of a whole school policy towards effective conflict resolution and clear strategies for dealing with both verbal and physical violence.

We believe that this approach goes beyond the remedial and the preventative and that it educates young people in skills of 'emotional intelligence' (Goleman, 1996) that they will need increasingly as they face the challenges of their daily lives.

'Mediation began as an aspect of school life – a taught element – and has become something which they use as part of their everyday lives, as useful as language and maths. Their skills, at whatever level, have extended into their homes and lives outside school.' (Sarah Hodgson, Behaviour Management Co-ordinator, Adderley J.I. School, Birmingham)

A social psychological approach to bullying

Social psychology has its origins at the start of this century (McDougall, 1908) and has been growing as a discipline ever since, with Kurt Lewin (1948) being the first fully to appreciate the previously underestimated influence of any group in shaping the psychology of individuals who are a part of that group. During the 1960s social psychology came into its own and influenced many other areas of study, including, amongst others, business management, feminism and education.

We believe that any long-term strategy to reduce bullying has to work with what Lewin (Lewin, Lippit and White, 1939) called 'group process' and that the culture and norms of the group will have far more influence on whether bullying takes place, than the psychological make-up of individual children and adults in the school. If the cultural norm of the school within its community is that bullying is part of the rough and tumble of life and a natural part of growing up, then it will be extremely hard to eradicate. If, however, a majority of adults and pupils in a school and the school's wider community support a culture which does not accept the inevitability of bullying, then individuals within that community are empowered to take action against it, within their own particular sphere of influence, knowing that their voices echo a common consensus.

In summary then, we are suggesting that teachers should not be satisfied with putting an arm around the 'victim' and wagging a finger at the 'bully', but that they work with the class or year group and adopt a whole-school approach to improve the quality of relationships. As an added bonus, if teachers create an environment that minimises bullying and maximises positive self-image, research has shown that this will also raise standards and create a successful learning environment (Gibby and Gibby; 1976, Hartley, 1986).

Developing positive relationships as a whole-school approach

Research attempting to explain the failure of the 1944 Education Act to bring about equality of opportunity argued that the major determinants of educational success were social circumstances, motivation, the family and home rather than teachers and the curriculum (Halsey, 1972). This led many educationalists to take a pathological view of the influences of home life over school life. More recent research challenges this overly negative view of education outcomes and demonstrates that programmes of social and emotional skills learning can and do have significant and lasting effects upon the skills and attitudes of young people. Where groups of pupils have participated in focused active learning programmes which give opportunities to understand, try out and internalise alternative social and personal skills, a measurable change in social interaction and empathy have resulted.

Our own observations and firsthand experience of the outcomes of this process of social and emotional education (particularly when it is in train as a whole-school approach) leave us in no doubt about its transforming nature. As early as a half term into their weekly sessions, staff comment that they can 'feel' the difference in a class of pupils. An atmosphere of inclusiveness, co-operation, positive attitudes and happiness is almost tangible. There ought to be an instrument to measure scientifically the presence of certain elements such as these in the atmosphere of a room! As it is, early indications from more traditional forms of evaluation (pupil and staff interviews, questionnaires, entries in accident and incident books, numbers of pupils referred or 'on report' for bullying or aggressive behaviour) strongly indicate growing social and emotional skills amongst pupils. The success of this programme of curriculum work, however, depends upon a genuinely holistic approach which views the component parts – teaching style, behaviour management style, learning style, learning environment and content – as transducers through to emotional maturity, autonomy and social responsibility.

It is commonly accepted that parenting and teaching styles, if they remain overly didactic and directing, can block the growth of independence and result in infantilism, where the individual relies on others to service their needs, to tell them what to do and how to behave. Similarly, an unremitting authoritarian approach blocks the development of an internal locus of control. Where young people have all their judgements and operating codes set for them externally, it is easy to see how they may more easily succumb to power of another kind in the form of pressure to engage in acts of verbal or physical violence perhaps, or in the form of bullying to gain status and control. It is ironic to think that the seeds of bullying and aggressive behaviour may be sown by caring parents and teachers who are doing their best to impose and maintain standards of good behaviour in their homes and schools. In our anxiety to 'stamp out' undesirable behaviour and qualities, we may invest too little of our time and energy in helping our children or pupils to learn desirable ones; disproportionately shouting about the negative things rather than 'shouting about' or giving attention to what is attempted positively or successfully. As Robinson and Maines (1994) point out:

> When a pupil gets a Maths problem wrong, our first strategy is to teach. When it is the behaviour that is wrong, we tend to criticise or punish.

This creates a learning environment hostile to the very things we are seeking to encourage. The damaging effects of this can be to lock individuals or whole groups into a cycle of self-prophesying poor performance or behaviour, and can lead to deterioration in self-esteem, the lowering of expectations, the reinforcement of stereotyping and labelling, and provide fertile ground for conflict and bullying behaviour.

Group dynamics and human relationships are, more often than not, ignored or left to chance in the drive to deal with curriculum content. Instead of becoming an integral part of the process of approaching each subject, the quality of pupil to pupil and pupil to adult interaction is likely to be missing from both learning needs analysis and curriculum content. Lecturing and proselytising about desired conduct, values and social skills is no substitute for the opportunity to rehearse these and have support in putting them into practice. Our experience has lead us to believe firmly in experiential learning and in the efficacy of groupwork. The power of peer group pressure can be harnessed to provide unequalled support for positive interaction, inclusiveness and equal opportunities.

Some teachers tell us that they have not had support in knowing how to approach and develop the social and emotional interaction of their pupils, or to derive the content of personal and social education from their observations of the needs of the group. Teachers need both a clear structure for this work and an understanding of how to facilitate this rich and complex process.

In summary, we are suggesting an approach which combines a positive environment in which a sense of self-worth and achievement can flourish; a conscious drive to improve group cohesion and inclusivity; to develop pro-social skills, with opportunities to rehearse alternative language and behaviour safely, to make real choices and exercise responsibility. Nowhere have we seen self-determination and mutual aid flourishing so well as in a peer mediation service.

Peer mediation: what it is and how it works

Peer mediation services need to be more than a 'bolt-on' feature, they need to be included in the School Development Plan and be written into school policies on Behaviour management, Anti-bullying, Pastoral care, etc. Peer mediation affords a genuine opportunity for pupils to exercise empathy and responsibility towards other pupils experiencing problems. These problems if dealt with swiftly through peer mediation can prevent the kind of escalation that leads to violent and bullying behaviour. The 'peer' in peer mediation can either refer to a small number of pupils within a year group who are trained to offer a service in pairs to others of the same age, or it can indicate that the service is run by older pupils in support of younger pupils throughout the school, or it can refer to a team made up of pupils drawn from across the year groups.

Pupils will normally have covered foundation work in conflict resolution and have had an introduction to the mediation process before they nominate themselves or others for further training. In the Catalyst model (Robinson and Stacey, 1996) this training takes place off-timetable over three full days. An intensive period of time such as this allows for team building and proper rehearsal of counselling skills but more importantly it allows young people the opportunity to develop their own guidelines for effective practice and to design their own service. Included in this training will be the members of staff who are to support the peer mediators throughout the year, lunch-time supervisors and any other adults or ancillary staff offering their support (Education Social Workers, School Nurse, secretarial staff, parents, governors, home–school liaison workers, etc.).

Decisions need to made not only about what sort of problems are appropriate for pupil mediators to deal with, how pupils access the service and whether referral is through adults, but about the finer details of rotas and responsibilities for running the scheme from day to day. In many models the service takes place at lunch-time four times a week. Some choose to withdraw into a quiet room or private corner, whilst other services operate outside in play areas at a designated spot. We have become familiar with many mediation trees, benches and gates!

The level of publicity and support from staff can determine whether a mediation service will stand or fall. In the schools where the services have been most successful the staff, including the lunch-time supervisors, have had at least one in-service training session after school, dedicated to peer mediation, and ideally a full training day. One of the best examples of this was when the pupil mediators themselves came in on a training day and taught the whole staff mediation skills. If staff have full awareness of what the process involves they are then able to make full use of voluntary referral slips which can be kept in their registration folders. Other successful initiatives have ensured that a high profile is maintained throughout the year. Pupils themselves are in a best position to know how to market and advertise their service amongst their peers, but will benefit from a partnership with I.T., Media Studies, Art, Drama and Business Education Partnership. Here is an opportunity to use photographs, video footage, posters and presentations, parents and governors meetings, word of mouth strategies (e.g. undertaking to tell ten people each who are in turn asked to tell ten other people), newsletters and input into PSE or Circle Time in other classes, to launch the service and maintain a high profile. Many peer mediation schemes give themselves a clear identity, choosing names (Trouble Busters, Helping Hands, Untanglers), logos, slogans ('Release the peace and be strong') and forms of identification such as baseball caps, badges and sweatshirts which allow them to be easily identified when on duty.

Although peer mediators need to have ownership of their service and make the decisions and choices about the way in which the service runs, they need regular adult support and supervision. This varies according to the age of the pupils involved, but all will need a weekly team meeting to debrief, to share experiences and to keep up a regular programme of review and development.

The burden entailed in providing regular support for the mediators will be lessened if it is a shared responsibility between more than one member of staff, and if the staff members involved feel confident in their own mediation skills and in the level of expertise they can bring to support sessions with the pupil team.

It is rare for any service to work perfectly from the word go. Even the most established schemes (3 or 4 years) need modifying or altering completely as the needs of the users change over time. Some schools in Birmingham experience a falling-off in the use of peer mediators as the curriculum work takes root and mediation becomes a familiar enough process for pupils to sort out problems early on, between themselves, without recourse to peer mediators. There will never be a time when conflict between pupils vanishes altogether, but peer mediators may eventually need to change the focus of their service to one, for example, where they promote positive play at primary school level or become a source of information and referral at secondary level.

The supporting curriculum

The skills which pupils need in order to be able to offer and use a peer mediation service are varied. They need the ability to express individual thoughts, feelings and points of view, the ability to accept the validity of opposing or conflicting opinions and the ability to use assertive language. They need to be able to listen with empathy and repeat in summary what has been said, to be able to affirm others and accept affirmation, identify feelings and cope with them, control impulse and understand responses. Specific conflict resolution skills include the ability to attack the problem and not the person, to separate issues and value judgements, to understand and own needs, and to brainstorm and evaluate creative solutions. Help in developing all of these skills can be provided by a programme of curriculum work integrated into school provision and policy as an ongoing part of the process of education .

We have adapted the iceberg principle first developed by Prutzman (1988) to give shape and coherence to the curriculum content (Robinson and Stacey, 1996). The model (Figure 7.1) shows how effective problem

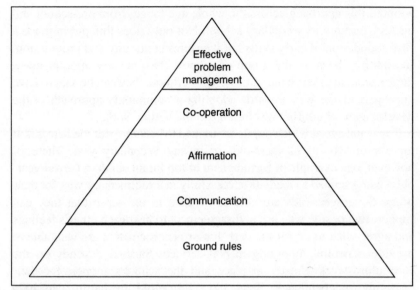

Figure 7.1

management is merely the tip of the iceberg, supported by the three core skills below. By using these broad areas to develop a range of curriculum activities an extended programme of work can be undertaken as an ongoing part of the curriculum, rather than as a brief intervention.

The curriculum programme always begins with foundation work to create a positive empowering climate. This is done using Circle Time (Bliss, Robinson and Maines, 1995) which is an interactive process supported by firm ground rules in which pupils are required to listen with respect to each other and to take turns in speaking. A sandwich of whole group 'go-rounds' (as pupils refer to the turn taking round the circle), are interspersed with pairwork, small groupwork and games or active learning. In a spiral curriculum, work at each phase is tailored to the developmental stage of the pupils and the learning needs of the group and of individuals within the group. The skills and concepts which enable a non-violent, creative approach to conflict resolution are established at each phase. The starting point is always to establish properly functioning ground rules where young people listen to each other with respect, take turns to speak, accept and include everyone and learn to operate as a member of a group. For some pupils, reaching these early targets will be a major achievement which will do a great deal to improve the quality of relationships and create a positive climate for learning.

Pupils of all ages are able to develop competencies in communication, affirmation and co-operation. It is never too early to start this curriculum process. The Saltley Plus Consortium of schools in Birmingham have adopted this approach across the whole age range, from pre-school and nursery through to secondary school. Not only does this put in place a firm foundation of early skills but it ensures continuity and progression. In addition, because the group of schools (two nursery, nine primary, three secondary) serve the same neighbourhood, they can be said to have gone part of the way towards adopting a community approach to the development of conflict resolution and mediation work.

The usual age at which pupils are trained to become peer mediators is at top Junior (10- to 11-years-old) or in any Secondary year. There is, however, one example in Birmingham of top Infant children (seven-year-olds) being trained to mediate successfully in a rudimentary way for their peers. Seven-year-olds are able to mediate in the sense that they can support two people who are in disagreement to hear each other's feelings and agree what to do for the best. Junior peer mediators are well able to provide a neutral, non-judgemental service. Success depends on the curriculum work already in place and the school's support for their emerging independence. Ten- and 11-year-old mediators can help disputants to understand what the problem is about, appreciate each other's point of view and choose a way forward that will change things for the good of both. All age groups at secondary phase can mediate successfully for their peers. With increasing age and maturity comes increasing perception and sophistication, and the ability to reach underlying issues as well as to identify unexpressed needs. A mediation between primary pupils may be over in a matter of minutes. Older pupils may need recourse to several sessions of mediation before reaching a resolution. Mediation between adults often averages six hours in total. The process of mediation, however, is broadly similar no matter what the context of the conflict is, or the ages of those involved. It follows a framework which begins with a reminder that the role of the mediator is to be a neutral facilitator so that whilst they will be helping both people to reach agreement they will not be making judgements, giving advice or offering solutions. For easy assimilation the process is taught as a series of steps (Figure 7.2), although in reality the steps are often revisited in a cyclical fashion which soon becomes an intuitive process for the mediators.

We would like to echo Andrew Acland's words from *A Sudden Outbreak of Common Sense: Managing Conflict Resolution through Mediation* (1990) where he says, 'Mediation's simplest and most important virtue is that it works'. He goes on:

> evidence from the United States suggests that 80 per cent of mediations are successful on the day, and another 10 per cent lead to settlement within the following month.

Step 1 Introductions
Mediator's role and ground rules agreed.

Step 2 Problems and feelings
Each heard in turn. Reflective listening and open non-judgemental questioning used.

Step 3 Conciliation
Disputants helped to see both sides, acknowledge the other's feelings and identify the main issues as needs.

Step 4 Choices
A brainstorm of suggestions, offers and requests, including negotiation and compromise.

Step 5 Agreement
A mutually acceptable way forward.
Action planning for the immediate future.
Long-term action and opportunity to reassess agreement.

Figure 7.2

He speaks of mediation's cost effectiveness in commercial and industrial dispute resolution. In schools, one of the most costly and precious commodities is teacher time. Mediation can help take some of the pressure away from the time-stressed teachers and managers; and can resolve conflicts simply and swiftly, without the complications, delays and often unproductive effects of more directive intervention. Mediation provides a powerful yet simple tool for turning disputes into harmony and growth.

Conflict resolution in the home, school and community

After the pessimism of the 1960s concerning the effectiveness of school-based programmes to improve social and emotional skills, and the research of the 1980s suggesting that schools can make a difference, we believe that the challenge of the 1990s and beyond is in finding approaches that take into account the dynamics between home, school and community.

Catalyst's work in almost 100 Midland schools over five years has included a limited amount of work combining home, school and community, but there has been one piece of our work where we were able to be part of an indepth whole-community approach co-ordinated by Daniel Cremin, the Manager of the Galton Village Peace Project. Programmes which we delivered in two of the three local schools were reinforced and enhanced by a much wider community initiative with the community work supporting the schools' work and the schools' work supporting the community work in a consciously-structured way. Daniel used our help to explore and express issues such as crime, abuse, domestic violence, bullying, neighbourhood disputes, racism and victimisation, through a common language of conflict in both schools and the community.

The Peace Project was set up in 1991. It was commissioned by the West Smethwick Community Safety Initiative and funded largely through a variety of charitable trusts. Its remit was to reduce conflict and improve social behaviour, particularly amongst the young, throughout the Galton Village housing estate. It was required to do this by working with individuals, groups and organisations in the community, from individual school refusing youngsters, their parents and local schools, to the residents' group, and other sections of the community. Clearly therefore, a co-ordinated, holistic approach was essential.

The Galton Village Estate in 1991 was made up of over 4,500 residents, 50 per cent of whom were under 25 years of age. The unemployment rate on the estate was 79 per cent. Average household income was less than £7,000 a year and 46 per cent of families were lone parent families. In addition to this, three local secondary schools had recently become amalgamated, with all the ensuing tensions between staff and pupils, including some new racial tensions as the school population became more mixed.

The work to develop peer mediation schemes in the two local primary and secondary schools, together with their underlying raft of related pro-social skills, took place incrementally over a number of years, until the end of the project in April 1996. Ten two-hour sessions for lunch-time supervisors in playground management and positive play underpinned the peer mediation services. In addition, the Peace Project worked with ten families with a truanting child to support them in dealing with the causes and to successfully reintegrate the children into school life.

Other ventures within the community worked with the same issues of conflict, crime and empowerment. Over 100 people, experiencing problems of various kinds including domestic violence and abuse, sought counselling with the Peace Project which often worked with social services, Refuge Centres, Rape Crisis and Victim Support services. Twenty neighbourhood disputes were successfully mediated and residents were themselves trained in counselling and communication skills. Unemployed residents developed action plans to fulfil their potential single parents set up a self-help Gingerbread group and a women's group was formed. Over a two-year period a residents' group gave expression to the concerns and feelings of residents relating to the development of their estate. Throughout the Project people were encouraged to fund-raise and take ownership of each part of the community development project. As a result of this, concerted pressure from the community helped to secure a multi-million pound redevelopment of the estate. This had a huge impact on morale.

Whilst large-scale research was outside of the scope of this case study, the indicators are that this community-wide approach went a long way towards improving the quality of life for a significant number of adults and children.

'The Peace Project has helped me to bring myself out and realise that I do have skills to help and it is very refreshing.' (Galton Village resident)

'The services, programmes and training which the Peace Project offers, is clearly having a positive effect on the quality of their lives and strengthening the community.' (West Midlands Police Constable)

'I find that mediation has helped me a lot because I have made people be friends again and people have helped me. I find that co-operation has also helped me because it is easier to do things now than before.' (Year 6 girl)

'I feel good, because I used to have problems as well and I couldn't talk to no-one.' (Year 10 male mediator)

Conclusion

Shifting the balance of power from adults to children, from the individual to the group, from professional to community member, encouraging confidence in a range of social and emotional skills, offering tools for conflict resolution and supporting genuine opportunities to practise these skills, can create a culture in which bullying and other forms of anti-social behaviour are overwhelmed by more positive new ways of using power and influence.

Note

Catalyst can be contacted at 5 Cambridge Road, Kings Heath, Birmingham B13 9EU. Tel: 0121 441 1222.

Chapter 8

Developing pupil counselling and peer support initiatives

Maggie Robson

Introduction

This chapter will explore the development of pupil counselling and peer support initiatives within schools in order to tackle the problem of bullying. It is very important to tackle this problem from a holistic perspective – victim, perpetrator and community – for several reasons, which will be outlined below. In the brief space of a chapter, only an *approach* to the problem of bullying can be offered. For this reason, a detailed resource list is presented at the end of the chapter.

In my work as a counsellor, I often have victims of bullying referred to me. One of the themes that often re-occurs is the client's sense of being 'super visible'. They often feel that they have no where to hide, feel very exposed and on view all the time. They seem to have lost the ability to be 'one of the crowd' and often suffer panic attacks in public places such as the classroom. Part of their assumptive world seems to have dissolved. Murray-Parkes (1971) describes our assumptive world as:

> the only world we know and it includes everything we know or think we know. It includes our interpretations of the past and our expectations of the future, our plans and our prejudices.

Clients can no longer believe themselves safe, either physically or psychologically. To re-create this safety is a very hard task and one that is accomplished more easily with help and support. It is important that the whole school – teachers and pupils – help in the creation of safety, both psychologically and physically.

Clients frequently feel ashamed that they are victims. They often believe they caused the attack or attacks and believe they should have been able to prevent it. However, it is never the victim's 'fault' even if, as outsiders, we can see quite clearly why they may have been chosen. It is up to the whole school community to reassure the victims that it was not their fault. We all have the right to go about our business unviolated.

Clients often remain silent about their victimisation for reasons given above and also because they feel complaint or disclosure will make things worse. As a community, the school needs to give a clear message that bullying will not be tolerated and victims' rights, indeed everyone's right, to be unviolated will be upheld. Bullying occurs, often, because it is allowed to occur by the hidden messages that are given by the community: 'She asked for it', 'He's such a timid boy it was bound to happen', 'We don't approve, but if we interfere we will make things worse', 'It's a cruel world, the sooner children learn to fight for themselves the better'. Children need to be taught to respect themselves and others and to expect and receive respect from others. This does not happen in a vacuum, it develops from the ethos of the school community.

It is not only the victim who is affected by bullying, but also the observers and perpetrators of the bullying. Morris Fraser (1973) illustrates this idea graphically when he talks of a pool of frogs into which a stone drops and hits some on the head and hurts/kills them. What happens to those hit by the ripple – no scar therefore no help? Children who witness violence, physical and psychological, can be affected in the same way as the actual victim and yet because they have 'no scars' they seldom feel able to ask for help and are seldom offered it. Perpetrators can feel powerful when causing hurt to others. This power is disrespectful and there needs to be legitimate, respectful ways of achieving this feeling of mastery through personal empowerment built upon respect for self and others.

So, the problem of bullying needs to be tackled holistically, by the whole school community. This can be achieved through pupil counselling and peer support initiatives. These will be explored, in turn, in the following sections.

Pupil counselling

I firmly believe that pupil counselling can help but first we need to be clear about what we mean by counselling. McGuiness (1989) suggests:

Counselling involves the use of a wide range of skills within the context of a relationship whose characteristics create for the client an environment of such safety, respect and support that s/he finds it possible to take risks involved in independence and creative response to life's challenges.

This very broad definition encapsulates the important elements in counselling but possibly still leaves us a little vague about what counselling actually is. It is perhaps easier to say what it is not. Counselling is not advice giving, finding solutions for the client or persuading them into a course of action. Each of the 'nots' may be a very valuable aid to someone in trouble but is *not* counselling. So what do counsellors do? Rogers (1965) suggests that the counsellor's role is to stay with the client through their journey of self discovery:

Rather than serving as a mirror, the therapist becomes a companion to the client as the latter searches through the tangled forest in the dead of night. The therapist's responses are more in the nature of calls through the darkness: 'Am I with you?', 'Is this where you are?', 'Are we together?'.

The role of the counsellor involves deploying skills in order to aid the client through the dark, tangled forest. Although these skills can be seen superficially as those associated with a friendly listening ear, counselling involves much more than this if the client is to progress from feeling better from 'having got it off their chest' to real growth and movement.

Often a distinction is made between counselling skills and counselling. Charlton (1988), for example, suggests that studies have shown that counselling skills have been shown to enhance children's academic performance and that these skills are easily acquired. As Lang (1993) points out:

Counselling skills can be seen as both less specialised and less demanding. However, it is in some ways a misleading distinction as generally neither counselling without basic skills nor skills without relationships is effective.

So, how can schools help in terms of offering pupil counselling? I would argue that they can help in two ways. Firstly, by interpreting counselling in a very broad way and by integrating it into the ethos of the school and secondly, by offering individual or group counselling.

Let us consider these options, which I feel are not mutually exclusive, in turn.

An integrated counselling approach

This differs from the traditional view of counselling in that this is a whole-school approach rather than a one-to-one, or group, therapeutic relationship. Lang (1993) argues, with reference to the primary school:

> For counselling to be effective in the primary school the broader context in which it operates must be taken into account and it should be integrated into a whole-school approach.

I believe this is also true in secondary schools. This approach involves the promotion of effective communication and the creation of a safe learning environment for all – children and staff. This can only be achieved by a commitment to self-awareness by the staff, a commitment to the provision of a safe environment for all and a commitment to learn and use listening skills appropriately and effectively.

Effective communication skills involve being able to actively listen to each other without judgement, imposing our own views or allowing our own view of the situation to get in the way of hearing the other person. Research by Brammer, Abrego and Shostrom (1993) has found that it is the *quality of the relationship* that has most effect upon whether interventions are useful or not. They have found that certain 'core conditions' must be fulfilled for a relationship to be successful. These are described by Rogers (1957) and are:

(a) The ability to empathise. This is the ability to enter another's world and experience it *as if* it was our own, 'but without ever losing the 'as if' quality' (Rogers).

(b) Unconditional positive regard. This is the ability to communicate respect and warmth for the client as well as a commitment to offer help and a willingness to try and understand the client's world. Rogers summarises these conditions as 'the extent that the therapist finds himself experiencing a warm acceptance of each aspect of a client's experience as being a part of that client, he is experiencing unconditional positive regard'.

(c) Genuineness. This is the ability to establish a relationship in which the counsellor is 'real' and is characterised by honesty and openness. Rogers says this means 'within the relationship he is freely and deeply himself ... it is the opposite of presenting a facade, either knowingly or unknowingly'.

In order to create this relationship we must be able to offer and the client must receive the 'core conditions' of empathy, warmth and unconditional positive regard. Rogers (1973) suggested:

> I have come to trust the capacity of persons to explore and understand themselves and their troubles, and to continue to resolve those problems, in any close continuing relationship where I can provide a climate of real warmth and understanding.

The provision of effective communication and the creation of a safe learning environment for all in this context has implications for staff training and support. The basis for promoting an integrated approach to counselling in school is to promote self-awareness in the staff. There needs to be an environment created whereby it is not only acceptable for staff to relate their own feelings and experiences to those of their pupils but where it is encouraged and planned for – perhaps by regular staff meetings set aside for this purpose. Lang (1993) suggests:

> They might, for instance, consider their own childhood experiences of being labelled in relation to the current experiences of their pupils and go on to consider ways in which labelling the deed rather than the doer might be promoted.

Also, counselling skills need to be acquired. This is not a new idea. The Elton Report *Discipline in Schools* (DfE, 1989), recommendation 42 states that:

> Initial teacher training establishments should introduce all their students to basic counselling skills and their value.

Numerous courses are available throughout the country and skill development could be and should be an integral part of staff development.

None of this is possible without a commitment to establishing safety. Staff and children will not expose themselves in terms of self-awareness if it is not safe to do so and it would be very wrong to encourage such exposure if there was a risk of hurt. Bowlby (1988) likens the need for this safety to the needs of a military officer:

> For it is only when the officer commanding the expeditionary force is confident his base is secure that he dare press forward and take risks.

An integrated counselling approach takes commitment and resources but it can be achieved although, as Lang (1993) suggests:

The major aim is to enhance the well-being and development of all involved ... the support of pupils facing problems will be much better catered for within such a framework than as a result of a school response purely focused on the problem.

Alongside this integrated counselling approach, the traditional one-to-one counselling or group counselling can also help. The next section will explore this area.

One-to-one and group counselling

McGuiness (1989) suggests that:

counselling is a skilled activity, with a real potential for harm if it is practised by the unskilled and untrained.

Added to this danger, where counselling is practised in school by a suitable trained counsellor, is the possibility of role conflict. Teachers, quite rightly, have a responsibility to protect and control the children in their care, and this responsibility can cause conflict if a dual role is assumed. A teacher may not be able to refrain from judgement (and often ensuing punishment) if they are to perform their job professionally. Counsellors, given their objectives, must use the core conditions and refrain from judging and punishing. Therefore, there seems to be a strong argument that the role needs to be separate. That is not to say a suitably qualified and experienced teacher could not also be a counsellor, but to suggest the roles be kept separate and be seen by all to be kept separate.

Once the right person for the job has been identified, counselling can help, either individually, or by group facilitation. However, participation in this process must be voluntary – counselling will not work if the client is there under duress. They need to have a commitment to the process (Rogers, 1965).

Individual counselling can help by offering a safe place, physically and psychologically, where the client can explore and make sense of their experience and integrate it into their sense of self. Broadly, counselling normally goes through three phrases, an exploratory phase, an understanding phase and an action phase. These phases do not follow a rigidly linear pattern. Overlap occurs as well as cyclical movement.

The exploratory phase is when the client begins to explore their experience and 'tell the story'. McGuiness (1989) suggests the aim at this stage is:

> to allow the client to get to the point of saying with confidence, 'This is the difficulty, this is my concern, my worry'.

The next phase is understanding. This is where the client, after having defined the concern, begins to form some understanding of the meanings that it may have for him or her. With the counsellor's help, the client unlocks any distortions in their perceptions and explores the context of their meaning making. McGuiness suggests:

> The understanding phase tries to bring the client face to face with the distortions, encouraging him (or her!) to explore why such distortions are necessary. It is vital that the counsellor should not intrude on what must be a personal understanding for the client. Suggestions by the client to the counsellor simply offer an external perception; what must occur is that the client should be helped to move forward to understanding himself (or herself) on his (her) own terms.

The final phase is action. This is when the client, armed with new understandings, decides what action, psychological and/or behavioural, they wish to take, or refrain from. The counsellor accompanies them in this decision making and helps them to explore possible consequences.

The above is a very broad description of a counselling process and it must be remembered that each counselling process is unique and will depend upon the qualities of client and counsellor and the relationship they create.

One-to-one counselling can help in the way described above. However, there are dangers. Firstly, if not handled sensitively and discretely it can be used as yet another way of labelling the victim or the perpetrator as weak. It is essential that the ethos of the school values counselling for it to be effective. Arrangements also need to be made to protect the individual's right to privacy and confidentiality – within the legal and moral framework within which schools work.

Secondly, counselling cannot be viewed as a panacea. Individual counselling aims to empower the individual. In a society, be it school or the country as a whole, empowerment needs to be accepted. If the system is dysfunctional, it is very difficult for the empowered individual to change it without great personal risk. Counselling is not a panacea and needs to be set within a context of respect and care for the individual.

Group counselling can also be helpful, given the above provisos. Safety must be a key concern of the counsellor facilitating groupwork. As has been previously suggested, growth only occurs in a safe environment. It would be very damaging to invite members to expose their vulnerabilities and for these vulnerabilities to be used as weapons by other group members. As counsellors we are responsible, with the other members of the group, for the creation of a safe environment (see Robson, 1994).

The process of group counselling broadly follows the same process as individual counselling, but the whole group, facilitated by the counsellor, provides the safety and challenge that allows the individual growth.

Group dynamics play an important part in exploring one's position, role and feelings in a group. It can be particularly helpful to children, for whom peer identity is very important. The ways of working with a group, as with individuals, are many and varied, and a resource list is included at the end of this chapter.

Another way of helping children is through peer support initiatives and these will be discussed in the following section.

Peer support initiatives

Within a holistic system, peer support initiatives can be very important. As Tattum suggests:

> There are few things more relevant to a child than how people react to him (or her), it is not surprising that the reflections of himself (or herself) in the eyes of significant others plays a crucial part in the self-concepts a child acquires. (Tattum and Tattum, 1992)

The way these initiatives are organised are many and various. The 'No Blame Approach' developed in the UK by Maines and Robinson (1991) is an example of an approach in which a teacher takes the account of the victim's distress to a group of peers (including the bullying pupil(s)), some colluders and bystanders. Each pupil, through seven steps, suggests ways in which they will change their behaviour.

The anti-bullying pack *Bullying, Don't Suffer in Silence*, produced for the Department for Education, also includes similar initiatives and advocates a method of 'Shared Concern'. This is a counselling method the aim of which is to establish ground rules so that a group of bullying pupils can co-exist within the same school as their victim(s). The aim is to reach public agreement on reasonable behaviour and determine long-term strategies for its maintenance. They also advocate the teaching of assertiveness training to victims and report on the effectiveness of two peer counselling projects.

Cowie and Sharp (1992) describe a peer initiative which aims to help the pupils themselves develop strategies against bullying, within their own setting. They do this through the use of a 'quality circle' – a method adapted from industry which has the potential to offer pupils skills in dealing with problems in any context. The circle makes a list of all the problems they wish to tackle and moves through five distinct steps (see Figure 8.1).

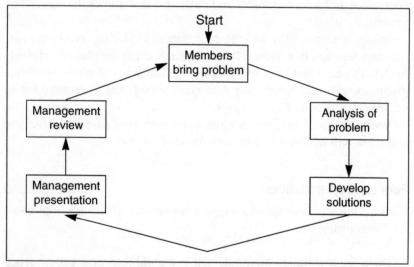

Figure 8.1: The Quality Circle Operation Cycle (Cowie and Sharp, 1992)

All these peer initiatives offer ways in which the problem of bullying may be tackled. However, I see several dangers, as well as advantages in developing peer support initiatives. The first danger is that the victim is in some way made to feel blame. To expect a victim to spell out the effects that the abuse has had on them could be seen as another form of bullying. At the very least, it expects the victim to expose their vulnerabilities in a way that most of us would shrink from. Also, the idea that victims need more social skills such as assertiveness training may be true, but again puts the responsibility back on the victim. As Morgan (1995) suggests, this approach can:

absolve the perpetrator of responsibility, leaving the victim feeling the burden of changing their behaviour to solve the issue.

The second danger, related to the first, is that the perpetrator is not expected to take responsibility for their action. Most peer support initiatives encourage the bullying pupils to be involved in finding strategies to solve the problem and while it is fruitless to engage in punitive punishment, a way needs to be found so that the bullying behaviour is abhorred and the person of the bully valued. Many of the peer initiatives do this and it is to be applauded. Bullying pupils need to be helped to see the consequences of their actions and to take responsibility for those actions.

The third danger I foresee is that power without responsibility can be dangerous. Children do need the help of facilitators whose responsibility is safety. It is not uncommon for bullying pupils and/or pupil 'courts' to decide on a punishment which in itself is abusive. A containment is needed. Shaw (1991) suggests:

> The aim of a good facilitator is to help the group feel safe enough, through the ground rules and structures used, to explore all their difficulties and begin to rely on each other, as opposed to turning to an 'expert' for help.

The final concern I have is that responsibility without power can also be damaging. A number of peer support initiatives advocate using peers, formally or informally, as counsellors (see *Bullying, Don't Suffer in Silence*, DfE (1994a)). This can be very advantageous to both parties but does lead to a question of how a peer can manage distressing material that may be revealed, without the power or support to deal with it. An example of this may be a student confiding in another that they are planning to kill themselves. This is a huge burden of responsibility which trained counsellors find difficult to manage. Are we not abusing children if we place them in situations where something of this nature may occur?

Conclusion

There is no magic solution to bullying. This chapter has examined two approaches to this problem, pupil counselling and peer support. Both these concepts seem useful and it is suggested that a holistic approach is needed. However, as suggested by La Fontaine (1991):

> Different approaches can be tried in different situations, given the variety of behaviour that children label as bullying. An entrenched problem may well need several approaches to produce an effect.

Finally, whatever we do, we need to do something. Evidence from callers to the Child Line devoted to bullying (Bullying Line) suggests that:

doing nothing is the worst reaction to being told about bullying that an adult can have. (La Fontaine, 1991)

Resources

Axline, V. (1989) *Play Therapy*. Edinburgh and London: Churchill Livinstone

Bond, T. (1986) *Games for Social and Life Skills*. London: Hutchinson Education.

Brandes, D. and Phillips, H. (1979) *Gamesters' Handbook*. London: Hutchinson Education.

Canfield, J. and Wells, H. (1976) *100 Ways to Enhance Self-Concept in the Classroom*. Allyn & Bacon.

Department for Education (1994) *Bullying, Don't Suffer in Silence*. London: HMSO.

Nelson-Jones, R. (1983) *Practical Counselling Skills*. London: Cassell.

Oaklander, V. (1969) *Windows to our Children*. Real People Press.

Pavey, D. (1979) *Art-Based Games*. London: Methuen.

The No-Blame Approach, Video and Insety Books. Lame Duck Publishing, 10 South Terrace, Redland BDS6 6TG.

Chapter 9

The 'Safer Schools–Safer Cities' Bullying Project

Graham Smith

Introduction

This project was initiated in June 1990 following a meeting between the co-ordinator of the Wolverhampton Safer Cities Initiative and officers of the Wolverhampton Education Department. The Safer Cities Project was a Home Office Crime Prevention initiative which aimed to tackle crime and the fear of crime in inner city and urban areas through local multi-agency projects. The project had three main objectives:

1. to reduce crime
2. to lessen the fear of crime
3. to create safer cities where economic enterprise and community life can flourish.

It operated through 20 local projects across the country, which were locally based and locally driven, with local people as policy makers, enablers and implementers.

Each project team consisted of three staff who co-ordinated and directed activity in their local area. In addition, each area had a steering committee which brought together representatives from local authorities, the Police, the Probation Service, voluntary and community groups, ethnic minority organisations, task forces, City Action Teams, business, industry and other local interests.

Following the initial meeting in June 1990, a steering group was set up consisting of various teachers and officers of the authority in order to oversee the project which was being co-ordinated by the author of this report. Although it was not anticipated that bullying was an especially large problem in Wolverhampton schools – that is, no larger than in any other inner city area – anecdotal evidence from educational psychologists, teachers and education social workers indicated that bullying was a problem which was affecting a large number of pupils to a significant degree.

The philosophy and aims of the project

The philosophy of the project was based on the following principles.
1. Bullying is present in all schools and is not acceptable.
2. Bullying has a marked and invariably harmful psychological effect on the victim.
3. Schools can encourage or discourage bullying through such things as their pastoral systems, codes of conduct, management styles.
4. Bullying is an abuse of power – this can be adult to adult, pupil to pupil, teacher to pupil or pupil to teacher.
5. Strategies employed by schools will be more effective if they are based on a whole-school policy.
6. Schools will be more effective in dealing with the problem if there is a sense of ownership of that problem.
7. A project is only worthwhile if the effects continue after the project is finished.
8. The project should be allowed to develop within each school at a pace to suit the prevailing culture.

The aims of the project were

1. To establish the extent and nature of bullying in a representative sample of schools in Wolverhampton.
2. To identify appropriate resources and intervention strategies and to make these available to Project schools.
3. To provide sufficient support for Project schools to enable them to implement strategies effectively.
4. To carry out summative and formative evaluation of the various strategies and resources.
5. To identify effective strategies and the processes by which these can be effectively implemented.
6. To disseminate the project results to all schools in Wolverhampton.
7. To disseminate the project results to a wider national audience.

The project plan consisted of three distinct phases.

1. June 1990 to March 1991 – during this phase the steering group was set up, project schools were identified, survey methods examined, the questionnaire developed and piloted, the initial survey carried out and survey results disseminated.
2. April 1992 to October 1992 and beyond – a resource pack was developed and provided for schools, in-school project groups were set up, INSET activities were provided for in-school co-ordinators together with ongoing support for schools.
3. November 1992 onward – this phase included project evaluation which, it was intended, should consist of a follow-up survey together with teacher questionnaires; dissemination of project results also came into this phase.

Methodology

The research design was to establish the extent and nature of bullying in a representative sample of Wolverhampton schools as a baseline, then to implement a range of interventions and strategies and finally to carry out a follow-up survey in order to evaluate the effectiveness or otherwise of the interventions employed.

From the outset of the project it was understood that it would be very difficult for the exact effect of each intervention to be measured, given that each school would probably take on a range of strategies and approaches to dealing with the problem – this in fact was the case, in that schools, once provided with a wide range of potential approaches, did indeed simultaneously implement a number of them.

The sample

Nineteen schools were chosen as being a representative sample of schools: 5 secondary schools, 5 primary schools (R–Year 6), 4 junior schools, 4 infant schools and one special school (MLD day school). In the initial survey in February 1991, 1,980 pupils were surveyed in these schools, each year group being sampled.

Schools were chosen to include all different types of school (11–16, 11–18, church aided, etc.) and with different ethnic and socio-economic catchment areas.

Following the initial survey, five schools dropped out of the project (the special school, two infant schools, one junior school and one primary school) leaving 14 schools to move forward into Phase 2 of the project. Consequently some 1,530 pupils were surveyed in the follow-up survey in February 1993.

Questionnaire

The questionnaire employed was the *Life in Schools* booklet format, first used by Arora and Thompson (1987, see the references at end of book) in a comprehensive school in Kirklees. A copy of the original booklet was obtained. This was modified in the light of discussion with teachers in Wolverhampton, and then piloted in schools in Wolverhampton. Three versions (secondary, junior and infant) were produced.

In secondary schools, the questionnaires were completed as a group exercise, this also occurring by and large for the junior age range; whereas, in infant schools, the booklet was used on a one-to-one basis as a structured interview.

The questionnaire was chosen partly because of the ease of use and partly because it allows children to determine (within the constraints of the items on the questionnaire) their own definition of bullying. Pupils are first of all asked to indicate whether the events on the questionnaire have happened to them not at all, once or more than once in the last week and, having completed this section, are then instructed to indicate by circling the item number, which items they considered to be bullying. A brief survey of teachers using the questionnaire indicated that they felt the questionnaire was easy to complete by pupils and that pupils understood what was expected of them.

Structure of the project

Each school that continued into Phase 2 of the project was asked to set up an in-school Project group – this consisted of five teachers in each secondary school, three teachers in each primary school, two teachers in each junior school and one teacher (generally one teacher, plus the head teacher) in each infant school. These groups were intended to be largely self-supporting; however, the in-school co-ordinator was offered considerable support by the project steering group and attended regular meetings with other in-school co-ordinators and the co-ordinator of the overall project. In addition, each in-school Project group was allowed time, through teacher cover being provided, to meet to plan their work in schools.

Phase 2 of the project was started with feedback from the initial survey being provided for each of the schools to enable them to target their work and to encourage them to feel a sense of ownership of the problem. This sense of ownership was enhanced in many of the project schools through a further period of data collection to establish other parameters of the bullying situation – such as who was bullying whom, where and when it was happening and what bullying was of most concern to pupils.

Guiding principles for the project were taken from the chapter entitled 'The Myth of the Hero-Innovator and Alternative Strategies for Organisational Change' by Georgiades and Phillimore in the book *Behaviour Modification with the Severely Retarded*, edited by Kiernan and Woodford (1975). These guidelines were as follows.

1. That the manager of the change effect should work with the forces within the organisation which are supportive of change and improvement; rather than working against those which are defensive and resistant; also to follow the path of least organisational resistance to achieve the goals, rather than confronting the resistance.

2. To attempt to develop a 'critical mass' in each school, through developing a self-sustaining team (*sic*) which is self-motivated and powered from within.

3. To attempt to work with the organisationally healthy parts of the system (i.e. the school) which have the will and the resources to improve.

4. To try to work with individuals and groups in each school who have as much freedom and discretion in managing their own operation and resources as possible – for this reason it was suggested that the project group in each secondary school should consist of year heads.

5. To attempt to obtain appropriate and realistic levels of involvement by key personnel in the system. As Georgiades and Phillimore state, 'often the best supporters of innovation and change are among the ranks of people just below the top, where personal commitment to the present is less and where the drive for achievement may be higher than at the very top'.

6. Finally, Georgiades and Phillimore state that 'frequent group meetings should be held in order to allow the team to discuss their own anxieties and doubts about the kind of work they are doing. Presentations and demonstrations of new techniques and processes as well as attendance at professional meetings and courses should be built into the timetable of the team'.

Intervention and strategies

A wide range of resources, appropriate to the age group, were provided for each of the project schools. Each in-school Project group selected their own priorities for action and planned their work accordingly. In addition to these resources, INSET was provided for in-school co-ordinators in the following topics:

- Bully Courts
- Developing play activities and play times
- The method of common concern
- Developing a whole-school policy
- The No Blame Approach.

Each school was encouraged to develop a whole-school policy as strategies were developed and implemented. Generally, strategies employed by schools can be placed into one of the following categories:
- drama and role play
- general awareness raising (assemblies, PSE sessions, etc.)
- developing play activities at break times
- restructuring supervision arrangements
- involving parents
- individual behaviour programmes
- the No Blame Approach
- developing skills of friendship
- bullying 'help lines'
- fast and unequivocal responses to identified cases of bullying
- art work and English.

Results

The results were from schools where the survey had been completed in 1991 and 1993 – for a variety of reasons some schools had incomplete sets of results and (apart from in one instance) these results were not used. In general the results do indicate that the *Life in Schools* booklet is a reasonably reliable questionnaire, the patterns of responses in 1991 and 1993 being very similar, therefore suggesting good test–retest reliability.

Tables of results

As can be seen from the following tables of results, not all negative 'bullying' items were analysed and compared. In each phase, only those high frequency items, as identified from the first survey in 1991, were analysed and compared.

Table 9.1: Secondary schools (Years 7–13). Percentages of boys and girls who indicated that the following incidents had happened to them more than once in the last week (all years)

Item	Incident	Boys (%)		Girls (%)	
		1991	1993	1991	1993
2	Called me names	28	25	23	20
5	Tried to kick me	10	15	4	5
7	Was unkind because different	6	10	9	5
9	Threatened me	6	9	2	3
16	Teased me	10	17	11	12
23	Tried to get me into trouble	9	19	8	5
25	Tried to hurt me	9	11	4	6
34	Tried to trip me up	14	19	8	10
40	Tried to hit me	17	12	6	8
	N =	448	489	438	475

Table 9.2: Primary/Junior schools (Years 3–6). Percentages of boys who indicated that the following incidents had happened to them more than once in the last week (all years)

Item	Incident	Primary (%) 1991	Primary (%) 1993	Junior (%) 1991	Junior (%) 1993
39	Tried to hit me	36	33	40	40
1	Called me names	28	32	34	43
24	Tried to hurt me	25	28	23	29
33	Tried to trip me	23	28	18	27
8	Said they would beat me up	20	16	17	17
38	Lied about me	21	20	16	38
22	Tried to get me into trouble	22	26	16	31
19	Had a gang on me	24	14	13	17
	N =	49	117	118	106

Table 9.3: Primary/Junior schools (Years 3–6). Percentages of girls who indicated that the following incidents had happened to them more than once in the last week (all years)

Item	Incident	Primary (%) 1991	Primary (%) 1993	Junior (%) 1991	Junior (%) 1993
1	Called me names	20	30	33	31
39	Tried to hit me	22	17	24	15
31	Shouted at me	18	29	21	37
24	Tried to hurt me	14	15	19	18
22	Tried to get me into trouble	14	22	12	12
33	Tried to trip me up	12	12	12	8
14	Stopped me playing a game	17	32	11	23
	N =	46	124	99	102

Table 9.4: Infant/Primary schools (Years R–2). Percentages of boys who indicated incidents happening this week (all years)

Item	Incident	Infant (%) 1991	Infant (%) 1993	Primary (%) 1991	Primary (%) 1993
1	Call you names	35	17	23	37
3	Try to kick you	44	47	38	18
10	Tease you	25	13	21	15
12	Get a gang on you	25	30	28	32
14	Try to get you into trouble	19	43	29	27
25	Try to trip you up	28	27	24	24
29	Try to hit you	33	27	29	15
	N =	32	30	51	41

Table 9.5: Infant/Primary school (Years R–2). Percentages of girls who indicated incidents happening this week (all years)

Item	Incident	Infant (%)		Primary (%)	
		1991	1993	1991	1993
1	Call you names	32	26	26	17
4	Try to kick you	20	23	21	27
6	Say they were going to hurt you	22	7	12	10
9	Swear at you	22	19	21	27
10	Tease you	13	19	19	19
12	Get a gang on you	15	23	16	15
10	Try to hurt you	11	16	25	33
29	Try to hit you	20	29	24	29
	N =	25	31	39	48

In addition to these calculations, the average percentage of reported bullying was determined, to provide an indicator of overall bullying across different items. The following tables detail these results.

Table 9.6: Average percentages – Secondary schools

School	Boys (%)		Girls (%)	
	1991	1993	1991	1993
All schools	12	15	10	8
S1	15	15	9	7
S2	16	22	8	11
S3	20	22	15	12
S4	14	12	6	4
S5	16	15	14	11

Table 9.7: Average percentages – Junior aged pupils (Years 3–6) in Junior and Primary schools

School	Junior				Primary			
	Boys (%)		Girls (%)		Boys (%)		Girls (%)	
	1991	1993	1991	1993	1991	1993	1991	1993
All schools	22	27	17	18	25	25	17	22
P1					38	23	32	24
P2					17	31	21	21
J2	24	28	17	19				
J3	28	25	17	16				

Table 9.8: Average percentages – Infant pupils (Years R–2) in Infant and Primary schools.

	Infant				Primary			
	Boys (%)		Girls (%)		Boys (%)		Girls (%)	
School	1991	1993	1991	1993	1991	1993	1991	1993
All schools	29	28	19	20	27	26	21	22
I1	45	30	26	25				
I2	32	28	21	18				
IP1					51	52	36	27
IP2					24	22	31	27
IP3					26	17	19	4

Summary of results

Generally, the following results were found:

- Nine of the 14 project schools showed an average reduction in levels of bullying over the two-year period from February 1991 to February 1993.
- Largest reductions were found in infant schools.
- Lowest overall average rates of bullying were found in secondary schools.
- Girls are consistently less bullied in all phases of schooling.
- There is a tendency for levels of bullying to reduce more for girls than for boys.
- The levels of bullying have been reduced, to a large extent, through reductions in one or two items, e.g. name calling, teasing.
- There has been an increase in reported levels of bullying on certain items, e.g. tried to get me into trouble.
- There is no clear connection between aspects of the school's catchment area and the levels of bullying.
- Levels of bullying for boys tends to peak on physical bullying items, and on social bullying items for girls – highest levels of bullying for both boys and girls occurred in Years 3, 4 and 5.

Conclusions

Clearly the most worthwhile reductions in the levels of bullying occurred in the infant age range. Exactly why this is is not certain; however, two infants' schools, where noticeable improvements occurred, took a whole-school approach to the project, involving teachers, midday supervisors, parents and pupils. Both also concentrated a good deal of time and attention on the playground, developing play times through improving the physical environment, introducing constructive games, providing play equipment and helping midday supervisors to improve their skills in managing pupils' behaviour. In one school attention was paid to enhancing the status of midday supervisors through involving the senior midday supervisor in a 'well done' assembly at the end of the week where certificates for good behaviour in the playground were handed out.

For girls in secondary schools, there were reductions in the levels of bullying in all but one of the schools; whereas for boys, there were reductions in the levels of bullying in only two of the schools. It is difficult to identify relevant factors which could account for these differences – there does not appear to be a clear relationship between the results from the school and the amount of work undertaken through the project. For instance, one secondary school, where there was a two per cent decrease in the overall levels of bullying for both boys and girls, had some difficulty with developing their work on the project for a variety of reasons including a change of school project co-ordinator half way through the project. It was noticeable, however, that this school had a well developed behaviour policy in place which may account for the improvement.

In only one other secondary school was there an improvement for both boys and girls. This school undertook a lot of work during the time of the project, carrying out considerable awareness raising in school through whole-school and year assemblies, through introducing bullying into the PSE curriculum and through drama and role play. Other successful work included a readjustment of playground rotas, some training of midday supervisors, the development of a bullying self-help group as well as the development of a whole-school policy.

Another secondary school had some success in reducing the level of bullying for girls. This school undertook, amongst other things, an interesting piece of work involving the use of a map of the school as a questionnaire, with pupils being asked to indicate on the map where bullying had occurred. As a result of information gained, supervision and duty arrangements at lunch time were altered. In addition to this, work on bullying was carried out in PSE sessions and awareness raising assemblies were held.

The size of the reduction in bullying in secondary schools illustrates how difficult it is to influence older pupils' behaviour on a whole-school basis.

Work carried out in junior schools included the development of the playground and play times, together with the development of PSE modules focusing on bullying. One junior school was successful in reducing the levels of bullying for both boys and girls, and undertook considerable work in developing play times as well as introducing bullying into the PSE curriculum.

The results generally indicate the difficulty that schools face in reducing the levels of bullying – this tendency seems to increase as pupils get older, presumably as a result of the behaviour becoming more entrenched and possibly more hidden as pupils progress through school. It may also be a facet of the size of school: the larger the school, the more difficult to take a whole-school approach – so essential to effective implementation of the range of strategies.

The relative success of the infant school suggested the importance of starting anti-bullying work at as early an age as possible – the focus on the playground at this phase of schooling also seems to have a worthwhile pay-off.

Generally the results indicate that bullying is the sort of behaviour that cannot be reduced through a piecemeal or half-hearted approach – effective responses to the problem are those that include everyone involved in the life of the school, that take into account preventive approaches to the issues, as well as indicating how to react to bullying situations. However, through discussion and interviews with in-school project co-ordinators, and comparing the work carried out in schools with the results, the following points were felt to be related to successful interventions:

- A small but enthusiastic project team should be set up.
- A senior teacher (ideally a deputy head) should be involved.
- Some form of survey should be carried out, ideally developed by the school, to act as a baseline and to encourage a feeling of ownership of the problem.
- Initial work should be on a small scale, perhaps with one year group or even just one class – but take a developmental perspective and plan for expansion.
- Involve midday supervisors and, especially in infant and junior schools, focus on play times.
- Develop a whole-school policy.
- Include preventive and reactive approaches.
- Keep the head teacher informed and involved.
- Involve pupils, perhaps through the school's council or a junior crime prevention panel if one exists.
- Involve parents, both in reactive and proactive strategies.
- Build on and relate the work to existing policies, e.g. discipline or equal opportunities policies.

Areas of school activity

Play times and lunch times

One secondary school used the ingenious device of a map of the school as a questionnaire and asked pupils to indicate on the map where bullying was happening – in this way they built up a thorough picture of danger spots around the school and altered supervision patterns accordingly through changing the staff duty rota.

Another secondary school also altered its playground rota to take into account pupils' expressed concerns about levels of bullying in certain areas. This school also carried out some training of their midday supervisors to improve their behaviour management skills and to raise awareness of the issues surrounding bullying.

One junior school received funds from the project for play equipment to be used at play times; they also involved staff in creating games to be used at play times and received an urban renewal grant to plant shrubs and create benches – through this work, they made a quiet area for pupils to sit in and take part in activities, such as painting and reading. Some work was also carried out with midday supervisors, e.g. the use of name badges, attaching supervisors to year groups. After dinner time, the supervisors report back to teachers, so that pupils see lunch-times as being an integral part of the day and are more aware of a consistent response from all staff to unsociable behaviour. The senior supervisor records disciplinary problems and incidents in a book and these are reported to the Year Co-ordinator. In addition, the school conducts in-house training with the supervisors where they raise problems and discuss possible strategies and practical ideas.

Another junior school set up a School Council which decided to spend some money on playground furniture, e.g. places to sit and tables. Pupils researched, costed and selected the furniture themselves.

An infant school targeted their work very much on the playground and developed systems for dealing with inside and outside play. Firstly, each supervisor targeted a child to watch out for – either a potential victim or a bully and used positive strategies, e.g. giving them helper badges, plus the use of praise and attention for appropriate behaviour. Midday supervisors were involved in training and attended teacher INSET days. On Fridays, the senior midday supervisor chooses a class of the week in a whole school assembly – this not only provides a powerful reward for children but raises the status of the midday supervisors in the eyes of the pupils. One dinner time a week, a midday supervisor is involved in a class for the last five to ten minutes of the lesson before lunch, so that pupils see midday supervisors as being an integral part of the school and are aware of the channels of communication between staff. In addition, boxes of games and activities have been assembled for use during lunch-times and pupils looked to improve the school environment generally through creating a litter-free playground.

A different infant school also focused very much on lunch-times and play times. The midday supervisor rota was altered, allocating two supervisors to each year group and attempting to keep one supervisor with one class for a month at a time to provide consistency and help build relationships. Considerable work was carried out on developing the geography of the playground and different zones were created to provide areas for organised games with supervisors, quiet areas with benches and a noisy area. In addition, the school developed a 'danger times' policy, which consisted of rules and procedures for those times of day that were identified as problematic, e.g. at the end of dinner time.

Developing whole-school policies

Some INSET was provided by the steering group for schools in the development of a whole-school policy on bullying.

The process often began with a series of awareness raising events in school such as assemblies or poster competitions. The in-school project group then took over the planning and drafting of the policy – a process which took some time to complete in some cases. There was often quite a lot of deliberation about the definition of bullying and exactly what behaviour to include or exclude.

All members of the school community were encouraged to take part in the consultation procedure. The following format was recommended to schools for the development of their policy document (with acknowledgements to the Sheffield/DFE Bullying Project).

Content
Aims
Definitions
Rights and responsibilities
Preventative action
Reaction/responses to bullying
Sanctions and rewards
Evaluation procedure

Process
Working group formation
Awareness raising
Formulation of draft policy
Implementation and communication
Monitor and review

One or two schools steered away from a bullying policy as a separate entity, but instead included bullying in their whole-school behaviour or discipline policy. There is clearly a debate as to which is the correct route to take. The author feels that it is important for there to be a separate bullying policy so that it has an importance within the culture of the school and is seen as distinct from a behaviour policy – some teachers were concerned about the use of the word 'bullying', partly because of the difficulties in coming to a clear definition. However, again the author feels that it is essential to use the word bullying, otherwise we are in danger of colluding with the code of silence that we are so urgently trying to break down.

PSE initiatives

One secondary school developed in their PSE programme a section on friendship called 'pressure'. This included bullying and dealt with such issues as peer group influence and when does peer group pressure become bullying. This was repeated in another secondary school.

One secondary school used the *Steps to Success* materials (Thacker, 1983) to help students look at ways of dealing with social problems in a problem-solving way.

A junior school developed a PSE programme which was divided into two sections:

Looking after ourselves – health and safety, sex education, etc.

Looking after each other – emotions, social issues outside school, stealing, vandalism, bullying.

This programme was timetabled so that all pupils were involved. In another junior school, a programme of study for Year 5 PSE was developed which included four lessons on bullying and associated issues.

Schools' councils and pupil involvement

A medium-sized secondary school in a relatively deprived part of Wolverhampton was the context within which a group of pupils started a bullying self help group which has come to be known as the Bullying Help Society. This group speaks to new pupils about how to cope with bullying and takes referrals of pupils who have been bullied and works with both victim and bullies in a conflict resolving, non-confrontational manner. The pupils have received training in basic counselling skills and also in using the 'No Blame Approach'.

In one junior school, a school council was set up consisting of one boy and one girl elected by their class in the upper school, who represent both their own and a lower school class. This council is instrumental in making decisions and is consulted to make it a part of the organisation of the school – for example, the school had an amount of money to spend and the council decided that playground furniture was required.

Drama and role play

One secondary school group of Year 8 pupils developed a play depicting a bullying scene and took this to feeder primary schools, involving junior children in deciding what action the victims should take. This was extremely well received by Year 6 pupils and was felt to have helped them feel happier about the transfer to secondary school – many myths about initiation rites were laid to rest!

A junior school video-taped pupil-devised scenes showing incidents of bullying. These were evaluated and discussed in class to help pupils decide on appropriate action.

Drama and role play was felt by schools generally to motivate pupils to explore ways of coping with bullying in a safe and non-threatening environment.

Other areas of work

The following schemes or activities were used by one or more schools:
- poster and poetry competitions;
- assemblies with bullying as the topic;
- group discussion using resources such as *Sticks and Stones* as the stimulus
- parent workshops to help make parents aware of warning signs and how to solve the problem;
- letter boxes in school for pupils to inform staff about bullying situations;
- developing assertiveness skills;
- developing reporting systems to allow consistent information about bullying incidents to be collected;
- work in RE on anger, respect and assertiveness.

Interestingly, even though INSET was provided regarding bully courts, no school took on this initiative – comments from teachers suggest that they felt that it did not fit with a positive behaviour management policy, that it would tend to label the bully and was generally open to abuse.

PART 3

HOME, SCHOOL AND COMMUNITY

Introduction by Delwyn Tattum

In addition to the home and school, bullying is a community problem and therefore requires a community response, whether the concept of community is applied as here to the community of the home, the community of school, the neighbourhood community or that of wider society. At the conclusion of the Introduction to Part 2 of this book, a Model 'Spheres of Involvement', illustrates the community of people who at one time or another may be called upon to deal with a bullying problem.

That bullying is a wider community issue can be seen in the dramatic growth in the number of organisations expressing concern. Among them are charitable organisations like Child Line and the NSPCC. Various professional organisations representing the Police, the Prison Service and the National Confederation of Parent Teacher Associations have recently published evidence of their findings. Among organisations representing employees – including teacher unions – there is growing activity, concerned about the way employer bullies employee. One union, the Manufacturing, Science and Finance (MSF), has initiated a 'Dignity at Work Bill', with the intention of safeguarding adults and young people from intimidation in the workplace. It is evident that the tackling of bullying requires a wider initiative for, unfortunately, it manifests itself in all forms of organisations wherever people may misuse their authority by badgering and harassing others – in the office, factory, hospital or even the armed forces.

The concept of communitarianism

The movement of communitarianism has its origins in the work of American academics, most particularly Amitai Etzioni (1995). In the United Kingdom a number of people were involved in launching a similar movement 'which would enable communitarian ideas to influence the behaviour of governments, organisations and citizens' (Tam, 1996).

But what is communitarianism? In the words of Etzioni (1995), it is 'a social movement aiming at shoring up the moral, social and political environment. Part change of heart, part renewal of social bonds, part reform of public life', for, 'without moral commitments, people act without consideration for one another'. To shore up the moral foundations of society, the starting point is the family, which is regarded as laying the foundations of moral education: and then the school, which reinforces the values gained in the home and which introduces values to those children whose parents neglected their moral and social teaching. Then there are what Etzioni describes as the 'social webs of communities', in neighbourhoods, work, clubs and societies. And these are 'the webs that bind individuals, who would otherwise be on their own, into groups of people who care for one another and who help maintain a civic, social, and moral order' (Etzioni, 1995). To achieve this moral ideal citizens have rights but also social responsibilities. It is a reciprocal relationship in which each member of any community owes something to all the rest, and the community, in turn, owes something to each of its members. As Etzioni writes, 'Justice requires responsible individuals in a responsive community'.

Recently, the government has expressed similar concerns and objectives. The National Forum for Values in Education and the Community was set up, following a conference in January 1996. The conference agreed that:

> although families in particular and society in general have the ultimate responsibility for the spiritual, moral, social and cultural development of young people, schools have a major contribution to make. (SCAA, 1996)

A Forum was established, representing a range of national organisations with the aim of identifying those values, attitudes and behaviour that school should promote. In their consultative document the National Forum put forward sets of values and the principles which influence behaviour under four headings, namely, society, self, environment and relationships. Their guidelines are reproduced in the Figure headed 'Relationships'.

This chart is shown because bullying is about relationships. An

RELATIONSHIPS	
Values	**Principles for action**
	On the basis of these values, within our relationships we should:
We value others for themselves, not for what they have or what they can do for us, and we value these relationships as fundamental to our development and the good of the community	• respect the dignity of all people • tell others they are valued • earn loyalty, trust and confidence • work co-operatively with others • be mutually supportive • respect the beliefs, life, privacy and property of others • try to resolve disputes peacefully

imbalance exists in the relationship when one party exerts power over another, and therefore has the capacity to make the victim do what she or he wants them to do – even against his or her will. The principles for action could be contained in any school's anti-bullying charter.

It is the case that moral crusades can be initiated by individuals as well as organisations, as witnessed in the case of Frances Lawrence, following the death of her husband Philip Lawrence, when he was stabbed by a youth as he went to intervene in a scuffle outside his school in Maida Vale, London, in December 1995. This was a murder that shocked the nation and called for a national initiative to tackle the corrosive value system that too many young people and adults subscribe to.

No doubt, some teachers will object to having a proscribed moral role as they may argue firstly about the difficulty of identifying an agreed set of values in such a diverse society as ours and, secondly, question their role as moral educators as there is already a danger that they are blamed for society's faults. And whilst the writer has some sympathy with the first point, he trusts that the National Forum's paper will identify areas of consensus and is strongly convinced that in the case of bullying no teacher can but condemn it as behaviour which violates the person and freedom of other members of the school's community. Schools are not moral-free zones, for one way or another moral education does take place in schools. For schools are social gathering places where youngsters talk about the music they hear, the magazines they read and the films and videos they watch. Thus the frequently irresponsible messages transmitted by the media will provide the values and attitudes adopted by them if teachers fail to take a firm stance in the development of responsible citizens in democratic communities.

Moreover, every school community creates its own climate and ethos by declaring what it stands for and its expectations for its members.

Teachers by their demeanour provide role models and every time a teacher disciplines an individual or class she or he takes a value position in declaring what is regarded as acceptable behaviour.

Has the problem worsened?

Having worked in the field of bullying for over a decade, one is frequently asked whether the situation today is any worse than 20 or 30 years ago. At present it is difficult to say whether the incidence of bullying has increased in the intervening decades because we do not have accurate baseline data from that time. The earliest figures we have about the incidence of bullying in schools come from Norway, where in 1983 they conducted a national survey. From questionnaires completed by pupils, they found that 15 per cent of pupils had been involved in bullying – six per cent saying they had been bullies and nine per cent that they had been victims of bullying. However, there is growing evidence that the Norwegian figures may be an underestimation of the problem. The results of small-scale, local surveys in the United Kingdom, other European countries, Canada, Australia and Japan would indicate a figure in excess of 20 per cent. This latter figure is confirmed by a more recent national survey in Ireland, where in the 1993/94 school year they studied 10 per cent of all primary schools and 27 per cent of all post-primary (O'Moore, 1997 forthcoming).

Alternatively, there is growing belief that the nature of bullying has changed and become more violent. It has also become complicated, damaging and extreme. A Canadian writer on the problem describes the change thus:

> Today's kids are growing up in an angry, fast-paced media-saturated, economically and ecologically unstable world, and their bullying seems to be crueller, nastier, callous. It's certainly more sophisticated and no longer one-on-one. Remember the weight-lifting ads in the back of comic books, the ones that were supposed to help the poor sods who got sand kicked in their faces? The best way to get back at a bully, the ads maintained, was to build up a good set of muscles. Today kids build up an arsenal. Or a group of friends. Or are simply prepared to grin and bear it. (Zarzour, 1994)

Teachers say that they have a growing concern about the increase in aggressive behaviour in their classrooms and about the school. They are equally worried about the nefarious activities about the community entering the school, as in the sale of drugs. In a recent survey carried out by the School Health Education Unit (Balding et al., 1996) 25 per cent of pupils aged between 11 and 16 years said they felt threatened and intimidated at school. Thankfully, only a small percentage of the 11,613 pupils surveyed said that they never felt so frightened that they ever carried weapons to protect themselves at school. On the other hand, 18 per cent of the 11-year-olds in the survey said they may carry some form of protection as they moved about the community. *Defensive* weapons, such as sound alarms and sprays were mainly carried by girls but *offensive* weapons such as blades and even guns were carried by 25 per cent of all boys. As pupils got older, an increasing number of both genders said they feared being physically attacked as they travelled around their neighbourhoods to visit shops, clubs or discos.

In the following chapters are illustrations of agencies other than schools taking the initiative and working with children and young people on preventative programmes to intervene in breaking the Cycle of Violence as illustrated in Chapter 14. For if we fail to intervene as early as possible in a positive way, the growing viciousness of bullying will result in the negative involvement of other groups in the community – for example, the Police, Law Courts and, finally, prisons. The worry is that *physical bullying* is becoming more violent as 'feet are used as weapons' to inflict grievous bodily harm. We are all aware of the increased concern about youths carrying knives and other offensive weapons, which the police may uncover during stop and search. Similarly, *verbal bullying* encroaches into the law in acts of racial and sexual harassment, and even the act of incitement may be evoked against bullies who incite others to acts of aggression or abuse, or even, as has happened on a number of occasions, to engage in petty theft or shoplifting. Finally, acts of *extortion bullying* will bring down the whole legal system on the perpetrators. And lest some teachers delude themselves into thinking that only minor incidents, like the taking of crisps and pens occur in schools, I conclude with a serious case of extortion which was reported in the press.

> Two 16-year-old male bullies appeared before Stafford Crown Court and were convicted of forcing four 15-year-old girls to hand over money on a regular basis. Payments began at £2 a week and rose to £5. One girl stole £500 from her mother's wardrobe as a one-off demand and another was forced to steal £2,000 from her parents. These school bullies were found guilty of blackmail and demanding money with menaces.

It is the case that if we fail to act as early as we can to stop bullying, it will escalate in its severity.

Chapter 10

Seeking to develop a
Whole Community response

Ted Welsh

This chapter outlines the experience of a community-based social work organisation's efforts to address bullying. It outlines the processes we have been through over a five-year period to initiate and develop anti-bullying work, the greater part of which has been undertaken within school settings. However, whilst the work in this area is still evolving, we have realised the need to extend the focus beyond schools as the only forum in which to address bullying. Our approach now encompasses schools, parents, other agencies and the wider community.

Background

Family Service Units (FSU) is an independent social work organisation. Its aim is to support families within the community. It is a national organisation which has 20 units throughout England and Scotland, each Unit being funded separately via their local authority and local fund-raising efforts. The Thurrock Unit was invited into Essex in response to a child's death in 1983. To achieve the broad aims of Family Service Units the Thurrock Unit provides an integrated range of services including individual work with children, family work, group work, community work, play activities and drop-in facilities.

While being aware of bullying as a recurring local issue for some time, the Unit's direct community intervention began as a result of learning that several children in families that we were working with were being bullied. These children were either afraid of going out to play or would run the short distance between school and their home to avoid other children. Black children in particular were being singled out in area that is predominantly white. Occasionally, family work or individual work included discussing bullying but a systematic team approach had not been developed.

In response to the problem a meeting was organised between their parents, the Police, the Youth Service and the District Councils' Housing Department. The local school was not involved at this stage as the meeting took place during the summer holidays. Our proposed solution was to run a short, therapeutic, group work programme for the victims. The intention was to enable those being bullied to begin to come to terms with their experiences and develop strategies to reduce the effects of the bullying. For several years the Thurrock Family Service Unit had been successfully operating a similar group work programme for children who had been sexually assaulted.

However, due to other work commitments and resource constraints, this was not where our intervention began. Looking back, if we had done so, it would have been a mistake, because it would have only concerned itself with dealing with the aftermath and would have failed to act in a more preventative way that would deal with the origins of bullying.

School-based work – the beginnings of a community-based approach

The anti-bullying work was eventually initiated, utilising a four-month student placement and focused upon, what was loosely termed, a 'preventative educational model'. This entailed working with children within a local primary school to develop their awareness of what bullying is and its effects upon victims. The school recognised bullying as an issue, though perhaps not as a major problem, and gave full co-operation to our working within the school. From the school's perspective this represented a valuable additional resource not normally available due to other demands on teachers' time. It is important to stress though that working within the school was not seen as a means of addressing a school problem but more of a convenient base from which to address a community issue.

Unfortunately, the initial project ended along with the student placement and the following 18 months were spent trying to secure funding to develop the work. This proved extremely difficult but eventually funding was secured through a literary evening with former hostage John McCarthy and Jill Morrell and a part-time worker was appointed to establish the Rainbow Anti-Bullying Project.

The Project represents our most significant direct intervention to date. Following the previous school-based work the aims became more specific:

- Raising awareness of what bullying and abusive behaviour are through direct work in schools and play groups.
- Breaking the cycle of secrecy that enables bullying and abuse to continue (this was heavily influenced by the Unit's work around child sexual assault).
- Making children aware of strategies which might help in keeping themselves safe.
- Exploration of ways to equip children to respond to some of the mixed messages they receive from adults – for example, hit back/don't hit back.
- Teaching children to be assertive.

Two important influences on the work of the Rainbow Project were the concepts of a 'Whole-School Approach' (Tattum, 1993) and the 'No Blame Approach' (Maines and Robinson, 1991). The former aims to involve all those working with the school (including parents), and represented, for us, a move away from awareness raising to developing strategies for dealing with specific situations. Equally influential was the incorporation of the 'No Blame Approach', which also moves away from the focus on the bully and the victim, reduces the emphasis on punishment, and instead enables the issues to be brought out into the open with a wider group of people. Thereby the cycle of secrecy is broken, and allows 'bystanders' or 'silent colluders' – that is individuals who either allow bullying to go unchecked or who are adversely affected as a result of witnessing bullying – to be brought into the solution.

Leading on from the whole-school approach, the Rainbow Project worked with schools in developing short-, medium- and longer-term strategies to respond to bullying. This included work on reviewing their policies and structures, to develop and improve them gradually. Great efforts were made to recognise the skills and abilities of staff, so that all could work together on a system that was both acceptable and practical. The Rainbow Project Worker also held sessions with teachers, non-teaching staff and governors, aimed at raising awareness and identifying training needs.

Initially, a group of Year 6 pupils designed and distributed a questionnaire throughout the school. Results of the questionnaire showed that of the children who responded:

66 per cent said they had been bullied in the last month;

53 per cent said bullying was so bad at times that they did not want to go to school;

32 per cent said they had been bullied more than twice in the last month;

51 per cent said they had been bullied at lunch-time;

30 per cent said they had been bullied in the playground.

The direct work with children took the form of circle time, the use of exercises to promote self-esteem and drama sessions. Prior to the appointment of the Rainbow Project Worker we had not fully been aware of the type of skills that would most benefit the anti-bullying work. We have subsequently come to appreciate drama as an extremely valuable medium for issue-based work. It allows the exploration of the emotions surrounding bullying to be explored in creative and imaginative ways. In addition, role play is a good way of helping children to devise and practise strategies to deal with bullying situations.

A particularly innovative element of the work was developed in the playground. In consultation with staff, pupils and midday assistants a 'Yellow Brick Road' was painted around another school's play area to prevent children going into difficult to supervise spaces. This was completed by a community artist and pupils from the school, and had 3-D bridges at key points where it was safe to cross, e.g. into the toilets and dinner hall. The 'Road' addressed two needs – it created an enclosed playing area which was supervised, as well as being an interesting play addition to the playground. As the school questionnaire had earlier highlighted that over 30 per cent of children had been bullied in the school playground, the creation of this safe area was significant. It emerged, however, that great care needs to be taken to ensure that another message is not given – that outside of the 'safe area' children are fair victims to bullies.

Other aspects of the school-based work included the establishment of a School Council as part of the Anti-Bullying Campaign. Pupils were elected and meetings were held to discuss aspects of school life and make recommendations to staff. A parents meeting was also held to launch a pamphlet called 'Talking Together' which outlined the school's procedures in tackling bullying. A merit award was received by the Unit from the Essex Child Protection Committee, in recognition of the work undertaken in 1994–5. Overall, the school-based work was successful.

Limitations of school-based approaches and issues raised

Work within schools is something we continue to develop. Currently this has been in the form of a joint initiative with the Youth Service and Refugee Council as a means of tackling racism against refugees. A part-time worker has been employed to undertake anti-discriminatory work within schools. A worker was also employed nationally by FSU, and part of his brief was to pilot strategies to maintain anti-bullying work within schools. This included pupil support groups and integrating material into the school curriculum. However, there are limitations to school-based work and we have become aware that schools cannot deal with bullying in isolation.

Alongside the work in schools, Thurrock FSU social workers had an increasing number of children referred for individual or family work because of behaviour problems in school (particularly boys). It was as if the staff's awareness of difficult behaviour and perhaps issues outside of school was being raised, and hopefully this will help to prevent the need for children to be excluded from school at such an early stage. The Unit offered some individual and family work, and also ran groups for particular boys to look at emotion and feelings, strategies for dealing with them, and raising their self-esteem. The work was useful to a degree, particularly as it included a few parents meetings too. But it did not necessarily deal with difficult situations at home or school, and had the disadvantage of focusing on a child's behaviour which may in fact be a symptom of a problem and not just the cause of bullying.

Schools are a major focus of a child's life but are only one part of the community. Children spend a significant part of their life outside of school. The education authorities cannot be expected to be responsible for what happens outside school well away from the school environment. Head teachers have expressed concern about the difficulties they encounter when children receive conflicting messages – for example, whilst schools are advocating non-violent conflict resolution methods, children are often being chastised at home by parents for not hitting back.

Also, for a variety of reasons such as lack of time, demands of the curriculum, or other priorities, schools vary enormously in their ability and commitment to addressing social issues like bullying. An early response to minor incidents and preventative intervention can help avoid escalation of bullying incidents and ultimately reduce the likelihood of more serious incidents. Ironically, schools who are better at addressing social problems are often reluctant to publicise the work that they are undertaking because of a fear of stigmatising their school. Sometimes, therefore, the initiative and drive needs to come from elsewhere, along with a need to begin to develop a community approach to ensure that there is an acceptance of collective responsibility and consistency within communities.

First steps in developing a community response

Multi-agency workshop

In trying to seek a broader perspective a multi-agency workshop was held. The task was to discover what work was currently being undertaken; to examine the effects of punitive and non-punitive approaches towards bullying; and to identify barriers preventing effective working together and potential ways of overcoming them. Participants included a head teacher, a teacher (who was also the former Rainbow Project Worker), an Education Welfare Officer, a neighbourhood police officer, the manager of the Youth Counselling Agency and representatives from FSU. We purposefully kept the workshop small in order to achieve practical outcomes. Regrettably we did not include parents which in retrospect we recognise as a mistake. Even so, this forum provided a useful start by beginning to share understandings of problems and drawing up incremental solutions.

Workshop outcomes

Although punitive responses to bullying were discussed, these are unlikely to offer a long-term solution. It was felt that by adopting the approach of focusing on punishment of the bully the issue is often forced underground as victims are frequently threatened if someone is punished. Such an approach fails to break the conspiracy of silence and does not address the role of colluders and bystanders. Instead, all present were in agreement with, and were already broadly implementing, the 'No Blame Approach'.

Barriers to implementing anti-bullying strategies

One of the factors preventing implementing the anti-bullying strategies was the fact that some individuals and organisations will not admit that bullying is an issue that needs addressing. Participants felt this may be for a variety of reasons, ranging from ignorance or a belief that bullying is a normal part of growing up, to an unwillingness to highlight issues which may be seen as reflecting badly on the organisation. The latter normally relates to schools, although many schools are active and positive in addressing bullying. A further obstacle within schools that was identified was the differing levels of confidence amongst teaching staff in their ability to deal with bullying.

Resources can be a major barrier in terms of time, money and lack of teaching aids. There is some material available, but those present at the workshop felt that locally produced, tailored material would be more suitable.

To employ a specialist worker to undertake direct work with children such as in the Rainbow Project is very labour intensive and expensive. The initial Project Worker estimated that to implement successfully a whole-school approach that includes parents could take two years. Given that there are 125 schools within our catchment area, widespread implementation through project work is not realistic.

Finding sufficient time is always going to be a problem. Whilst liaison and a co-ordinated response between agencies was identified as desirable, it was recognised that it inevitably receives a low priority in terms of other more immediate and work specific demands. For example, there was a problem in maintaining the allocated time for community policing, as neighbourhood beat policing generally tends to take a lower priority to other policing demands. Participants agreed that the police have an important preventative role and this could be best achieved through neighbourhood beat officers. Although discussing the role of the police, it remains unclear as to at what stage bullying becomes a criminal matter.

Developing a community approach

One of the major themes to emerge from the workshop was that individuals, schools and organisations within the community must accept a shared responsibility for implementing effective anti-bullying strategies. Where schools have developed positive behaviour policies it has been found that implementation can be easily undermined by contradictory advice to children from parents. For example, children are advised to fight back to look after themselves. On the other hand, when a school ignores bullying this can be just as counter-productive as parents advocating fighting back. When contradictory messages are being given, parents and community organisations can take the initiative to instigate working together to ensure a co-ordinated and consistent approach to the problem of bullying.

The belief that bullying is endemic makes the concept of developing a community response seem daunting. Inspiration can however be drawn from the field of community development which draws its agenda from individuals' immediate experience and the needs of the area in which they live. Collective action underpins community development as an appropriate means by which to achieve social change. Community development also seeks to encourage individuals to take more control over issues that affect their lives, and to participate in the making of decisions relating to them. Like school-based work it requires resourcing and is not an instant solution, but it is one way of minimising the feelings of powerlessness.

To begin to discover the attitudes towards bullying within the community a questionnaire was undertaken with adults. We were interested to ascertain people's views on bullying and to find out if they felt it had improved or deteriorated since they were children. This was only a pilot questionnaire with 20 adults chosen at random. The majority felt that the situation was the same as when they were children, although they felt there is more publicity today and 75 per cent said they felt bullying could be both verbal and physical. Despite the limitations of the questionnaire it was encouraging that most of those questioned felt that bullying was an issue that needed to be addressed.

Since the initial multi-agency workshop, efforts have been made to develop a co-ordinated response that includes parents by the establishment of an Anti-Bullying Steering Group. The purpose is to work towards employing a consistent approach to bullying, and to provide a forum for the sharing of information, knowledge, experience, and ultimately for the development of anti-bullying strategies. Originally the aim was to establish an independent organisation to address bullying so that no individual organisation's perspective dominated. However, as a result of the recent successful funding applications, Family Service Unit has employed two anti-bullying workers for three years and is likely to take the lead in the co-ordination of this work. In the long-term it is hoped that progress will be made through the co-ordination of multi-agency meetings and action between schools, voluntary and statutory organisations, churches, the Police and, most importantly, parents and young people.

One of the earliest functions of the steering group has been to raise awareness of the level and nature of bullying within the wider community. Working with the District Council and the local press (who produce a free newspaper which is distributed to all households), an anti-bullying newspaper supplement was produced. The supplement included work of both primary and secondary school children in the form of poems, cartoons, short punchy comments regarding the impact of bullying, plus a narrative account of one boy's story of how bullying had affected him. The purpose of the supplement was to publicise some of the positive work being undertaken by schools and organisations in the area and to raise awareness of bullying. We also wanted to highlight the negative impact that bullying has on children in a non-sensational manner. An important aspect of the supplement was simply to encourage parents to talk to their children about the subject and to challenge the belief that bullying is inevitable. Information on sources of help were also contained in the article. The newspaper supplement was a starting point but we need to work on maintaining awareness raising campaigns and publicise the work of the steering group by holding public meetings and the circulation of information and leaflets.

The Unit expects to develop the Rainbow Project considerably over the coming three years. The momentum of the steering group, openings in schools and the Unit's family, group and community work experiences, which can be applied to anti-bullying work means that a range of responses and initiatives will be taking place. For example, FSU and other voluntary organisations aim to develop a volunteer counselling programme for children and young people. The intention is to establish a recruitment and training programme for volunteers, and develop a system to provide ongoing support for them. We also hope to develop accessible resources and materials that parents and professionals can use, and a training programme for them that will support them to combat ignorance and ensure consistency in strategies.

Conclusion

Originally, we identified schools as the most convenient base from which we could develop anti-bullying work. This entailed Thurrock Family Service Unit working within schools to develop anti-bullying strategies and procedures for dealing with bullying situations. Drama in particular was utilised in direct work with children and is an approach that from experience we would advocate. However, there are limitations to school-based work, as schools are only one part of the community.

In the long term, therefore, if any strategies are to be effective there is a need to develop a wider community approach that incorporates community organisations and parents. Community development models have a lot to offer to anti-bullying approaches. The Thurrock Family Service Unit is still in the early stages of the work but beginning to find the direction in which it wants to move in collaboration with children, parents and the wider community.

Chapter 11

School Watch: working with pupils to make schools safer places

George Ball, Shirley Barry, Jim Fletcher and Charlie Naish

Introduction

School Watch is an initiative promoted by the South Wales Constabulary as part of its schools' liaison programme, and has the full support of education authorities within the locality. Its aim is to provide young children with the opportunity to improve their environment by taking responsibility for their behaviour and their actions. By encouraging pupils to accept ownership of problems and by allowing them to take control of the decision-making process. School Watch seeks to:

- encourage good behaviour and mutual respect amongst young people
- instil a pride in the school and its achievements
- promote safety in and around the school
- prevent bullying, racism and all forms of anti-social behaviour.

At present 21 police officers are employed by the South Wales force on full-time schools liaison, and these officers have become familiar figures in and around local schools. Attitudes to authority are formed early, and, in the absence of firsthand experience, young people can be susceptible to the stereotyped images of police portrayed on television and elsewhere in the media. Routine visits to primary schools improve the rapport between young people and the police, and provide opportunities for pupils to become conversant with their role in society generally.

Everything that School Watch attempts is, in the first instance, directed towards benefits for the school and its pupils. This philosophy is based upon the belief that advantages will eventually spill over to the community in general as pupils' confidence, social-awareness and levels of responsibility increase. Also implicit in this approach is a recognition of the demands and constraints imposed by the National Curriculum. For example, activities in which pupils participate provide opportunities for the development of key skills in the core subjects, such as:

Speaking and Listening
- making a range of contributions
- sharing ideas, insights and opinions
- exploring, developing and explaining ideas
- reporting and describing events and observations

Writing
- writing as a means of developing, organising and communicating ideas
- writing for an extended range of readers and in response to a wide range of stimuli
- writing for a wide range of purposes

Using and Applying Mathematics
- taking increasing responsibility for organising and extending tasks
- making and monitoring decisions to solve problems
- making general statements based on evidence that has been produced
- explaining reasoning

Experimental and Investigative Science
- turning ideas into a form that can be investigated;
- making predictions that can be useful when planning what to do;
- deciding what evidence to collect.

Additionally, involvement in School Watch has benefits for schools both in terms of school effectiveness, where it can make a significant contribution to policy and practice in behavioural matters, and also within the general area of school inspection, where a variety of extremely positive comments have been received by participating schools.

Establishing a School Watch Group

The School Watch programme began in primary schools in and around Barry, South Glamorgan, in 1993. It has since spread to the Vale of Glamorgan and Cardiff, and is currently being extended to secondary schools in these areas.

School Watch works *for* the pupils and *through* the pupils. Schools wishing to participate are invited to arrange for a visit by the local schools' liaison officer who provides pupils with an illustrated talk which explains the project's aims, its method of working, and gives examples of other schools' initiatives within School Watch. A committee of senior pupils (usually Years 5 and 6) is then democratically elected by their peers and charged with responsibility for managing and administering their own School Watch policy. A chairperson, vice-chair and two secretaries are chosen by the committee, which is advised and supported by the liaison officer and a designated member of the school's staff. The first requirement made of this committee is the writing of two letters, one to the Superintendent of Police informing him of the existence of the School Watch committee, and a second to the Chairman of the School Governors explaining the aims of School Watch and providing information on the existence and composition of the committee. The only other requirement made of the committee is for regular meetings with circulated agendas and typewritten minutes (see Figures 11.1 and 11.2). Matters of business are decided by the committee themselves and the other pupils in the school, who also receive advice from the liaison officer on the types of contribution that they can make.

Some of the individual initiatives undertaken by schools are discussed in the next section, while a summary of the achievements of one particular School Watch committee (prepared by themselves) is shown in Figure 11.3.

**VALE OF GLAMORGAN POLICE AND SCHOOLS
A PARTNERSHIP
School Watch agenda**

MEETING TO BE HELD:...

1. Apologies
2. Minutes of previous Meeting
3. Matters arising from Minutes
4. Correspondence
5.
6.
7.
8.
9. Any other business
10. Date of next meeting

Figure 11.1: Outline agenda for School Watch meeting

VALE OF GLAMORGAN POLICE AND SCHOOLS
A PARTNERSHIP
School Watch agenda

MINUTES OF MEETING HELD AT................................SCHOOL
ON...

1. Attendance
2. Apologies
3.

Figure 11.2: Minutes pro forma for use by School Watch committee

A regular feature of School Watch is an organised programme of conferences and presentations. Each term a participating school is asked to host a short conference for invited representatives from other committees in the area. The purpose of these local conferences is to encourage the exchange of ideas and to promote friendship. An annual School Watch presentation day is also held at which members of the various groups and their committees receive certificates and awards in recognition of their efforts. The presentations are taken extremely seriously by their communities, with local dignitaries making civic awards to reward notable achievements. Such occasions, coupled with local press coverage, have helped to establish and enhance the reputation of the School Watch programme within South East Wales, and guarantee its success.

Some examples of School Watch initiatives

As indicated earlier, the activities undertaken by School Watch are those which are proposed, accepted and supported by the children themselves. Projects can include anything from producing magazines to clearing litter from school grounds, although one of the most popular and appealing has been the provision of a School Watch Post-box, or 'Bullybox'. The post-box, which is often individually and imaginatively designed by the pupils, is placed in some central position such as the school foyer or assembly hall, and the pupils are encouraged to 'post' their ideas, complaints and concerns to the School Watch committee for consideration. The 'Bullybox' is similar in concept, although the main focus for mail is bullying. The letters received are often very revealing, with many concerns centred around friendship and exclusion. An 'airing' of the issues is often sufficient to resolve potential problems which might otherwise have festered and multiplied. Serious problems which cannot be dealt with by the School Watch committee are passed on to the head teacher for appropriate investigation and action.

What do the School Watch Committee do?

The Committee meets once a fortnight. An agenda is circulated before-hand and the meeting is carefully minuted by the secretary.

Letters from children are read out and dealt with. New ideas are discussed and some taken on board. The various sub-committees give an account of their work. Some of the things we have achieved are as follows:

1. *Set up a post-box for many types of mail*
   We are lucky in that we don't have a great problem with bullying. We get letters with suggestions for playground games, items to buy for use in the playground, news for the newsletter, and nominations for the friendship trophy.

2. *Raised funds to spend on equipment to be used in the playground at breaktimes*
   The playground can be a very boring place as there is really nothing for the children to do. If children are given something worthwhile to do there will be fewer incidences of bullying and rough play.

3. *Formed a rota of senior pupils who help the teachers patrol at breaktimes*

4. *Set up a special School Watch Notice Board in the assembly hall*

5. *Produced Newsletters*
   These keep the whole school informed of the committee's ideas and decisions. The newsletter also encourages children to write in with their news and suggestions.

6. *Designed our own logo*
   This can be seen on the badges our members wear to make them easily recognisable throughout the school.

7. *Designed our own stationery*

8. *Won a shield for Best Committee for 1993 which was presented at Dyffryn Gardens*

9. *Carried out a survey on wearing seat belts*

10. *Made a road safety video*

11. *Visited other School Watches in their schools*

12. *Given a 'Friendship Trophy' each half term to a child who has been a good friend to other children*

Figure 11.3: Summary of achievements – St Athan Junior School. School, Watch Committee

Other ideas which have travelled well, thanks to the regular conferences and exchange visits promoted by School Watch, include friendship partners (pen-pals), conservation areas, friendship gardens, and a variety of community projects. Typical of these is the 'Plant a Seed Project' which regularly produces a delightful array of window boxes and potted plants for local nursing homes and senior citizens.

One of the more ambitious projects to have reached fruition was undertaken by the School Watch committee of Gladstone Primary School, Barry, who designed, financed and built their own friendship garden. Having identified an appropriate site for the garden (a partly enclosed corner of the playground sheltered from winds and offering some privacy) the children set about producing a list of proposals for the garden's potential use and design. It was suggested that the garden could be used during break times as a quiet area for reading or talking to friends; as somewhere quiet to relax and possibly picnic; or simply as a place to 'get away from it all'. The garden could also be used on fine days for timetabled activities, as well as after school for club meetings and School Watch. The children identified benches, fencing, crazy paving, patio slabs, grass, flowers, trees and climbing plants as necessities, and ran a competition for the design of the garden. With advice, the successful design was translated into a working plan, while the quantities and costs of raw materials were calculated with the help of a local builders' merchant. The estimated cost of slightly over £1,500 did not deter the children who set about the task of attracting sponsorship for their project with vigour. The children's carefully thought out letters, which reflected their concern for the local environment and community, and which included copies of their plans and the itemised costs, won the support of a sufficient number of local business firms and individuals to make the garden a reality. The obvious pleasure that the pupils now derive from the careful and caring use of the garden is a fitting tribute to their achievement, and to that of School Watch.

Initiatives similar to the ones described above have helped to provide benefits for pupils, schools and local communities. Many pupils have achieved greater self-esteem, recognised the importance of citizenship, or realised leadership and organisational skills through the opportunities provided. Schools have become safer, happier, more caring places, with older children prepared to take greater responsibility for the welfare of their younger colleagues. Extra pairs of eyes and hands have proved invaluable in helping deal with vandalism, litter and bullying. Communities have further benefited with the greater social awareness of the children spilling over and influencing parents and families. Indeed, in one such instance the School Watch committee provided the motivation for their parents to establish a local Neighbourhood Watch scheme, thus making a significant contribution to crime prevention within their district.

Effectiveness of the School Watch initiative

In order to obtain a measure of the effectiveness of the School Watch initiative, the Countering Bullying Unit at the University of Wales Institute, Cardiff, and the Schools' Liaison Department of the South Wales Constabulary, have undertaken a questionnaire survey of eight of the participating schools. The survey, which was conducted during June and July 1995, involved schools of varying size and type drawn from a number of different geographical and socio-economic areas within South East Wales. The questionnaire, which was administered to some 1,369 primary pupils, targeted bullying, litter-spreading, vandalism and truancy. Pupils were asked for their opinions concerning the occurrence of each of these anti-social behaviours during the school year that was drawing to a close; whether they believed that such behaviour was on the increase or not, and reasons for any perceived changes. A high proportion of pupils reported seeing, or being involved in, acts in each of these areas (see Table 11.1) although it is possible that a number of the respondents may have been referring to a small subset of common incidents. Nevertheless, a major proportion of respondents in all categories believed that the incidence of such behaviour was on the decrease (see Table 11.2).

Bullying	Litter-spreading	Damage to school property	Damage to personal property	Truancy
65.5	86.8	35.3	39.7	29.9

Table 11.1: Percentage of pupils reporting experiences of anti-social behaviour at their schools

	Bullying	Litter-spreading	Damage to school property	Damage to personal property	Truancy
Less	40.2	37.5	52.4	55.0	54.2
Same	33.8	33.4	36.6	31.4	31.3
More	20.7	25.9	4.8	6.9	5.9
Unanswered	5.3	3.2	6.2	6.7	8.6

Table 11.2: Percentage of respondents indicating a change in the level of anti-social behaviour

When asked for the reasons for a perceived change in behaviour, the highest percentage of those pupils indicating a decrease cited the influence of teaching or ancillary staff. This was the case regardless of category. However, a pleasing proportion of the pupils stated that School Watch had been the main contributory factor influencing such a decrease. In particular, it is worth noting that in the case of bullying, the School Watch initiative appears to have been particularly successful, with 14.9 per cent of the sample identifying it as the main reason for a decrease as compared with 12.1 per cent for a decrease in damage to school property, 10.3 per cent for a decrease in litter dropping, 7.6 per cent for a decrease in damage to personal property, and just 1.0 per cent for a decrease in truancy. These responses, coupled with others which indicated a greater social awareness amongst the pupil population (e.g. 'Pupils have more sense now' or 'People have improved') and which may be partially attributable to the efforts of School Watch, can be considered extremely rewarding (Table 11.3).

	Bullying	Litter spreading	Damage to school property	Damage to personal property	Truancy
Influence of teaching/ ancillary staff	17.0	16.4	21.2	20.1	21.3
School Watch (mentioned by name)	14.9	10.3	12.1	7.6	1.0
Greater awareness (characterised by appropriate statement)	6.2	7.1	8.0	11.8	6.1

Table 11.3: Reasons cited by pupils for decrease in incidence of anti-social behaviour (percentage of respondents in each category

The effectiveness of the School Watch initiative can also be judged by an increasing number of direct references to its work within inspection reports produced under Section 9 of The Education (Schools) Act, 1992. Some examples of these are produced below.

A 'school watch' committee, democratically organised and impressively run by the children in year six, makes a significant contribution to good relationships and to the general ethos of the school. It aims to help children with individual problems and to try and prevent bullying. To do this it organises patrols of the playground at playtimes and tries to ensure that everyone is happy. A post box in the hall also allows hesitant children to share their problems privately. The system is working well with the children taking their responsibilities seriously. The school watch committee also shares in certain organisational aspects of school life. It helps under the auspices of Actionaid to collect a monthly subscription from the children to support Abu, a child living in Sierra Leone. It also produces a school magazine from the profit of which it subsidises the gardening club. The children are to be congratulated on their initiative in this committee. *St Athan Junior School*

Based on the guidance and initiative of the local school police liaison officer, the children have formed a 'School Watch' scheme.

Children's fears, problems or grievances are addressed anonymously through a 'Worry-box' which is housed in the library. This is checked daily by the teacher in charge and is acted upon immediately in discussion with the head teacher. *St David's Church in Wales Primary School, Colwinston*

Regular visits are made by a police liaison officer. A School Watch Committee has been set up and has won the Major's Shield for its work. It has encouraged the local residents to set up a Neighbourhood Watch Committee. *Cadoxton Junior School, Barry*

Prefects in Year 6 and other monitors have formed a 'School Watch Committee', which attempts to solve any minor problems notified through a 'worry box'. The group also makes decisions on minor monetary matters and has its own bank account. This arrangement provides further opportunities for responsibility to be exercised. Pupils show concern for others, particularly the younger ones, when they are upset. *Pendoylan Church in Wales Primary School*

A School Watch group of Year 6 pupils has been set up and has some influence in encouraging the participation of pupils in maintaining a safe, caring and supportive school community. *Romilly Junior School, Barry*

However, the overall success of School Watch is best judged by the children themselves, to whom is given the final word:

'We have been trying to sort out bullying. There was a problem with bullies but now, thanks to School Watch, there are no problems'. (Caroline, aged 11)

'The whole idea is to make school a better place from the pupil's point of view. We can come up with our own ideas and it really works!' (Daniel, aged 10)

Chapter 12

Tackling bullying and racial harassment in schools, children's homes and youth clubs

Gerry German and Sita Kumari

Introduction

Bullying and racial harassment are widespread and affect children, adolescents and young adults as well as older members of the community in rural and in urban areas. They are problems that spill over between school, street, housing estate and football terrace. Individuals are threatened, intimidated, isolated, rejected, injured, murdered even – and for the survivor the situation is made worse by the feeling that such appalling things can happen from day to day and year to year with nobody being made accountable or brought to justice.

As long ago as 21 March 1984, in a speech, entitled 'Racial Bullying in School', to the Reading Chamber of Commerce, the then Secretary of State for Education, Sir Keith Joseph, spoke about the 'particularly pernicious' effect of racially motivated bullying because of its wider attack on parents, family and cultural traditions. The Swann Report, *Education for All* (DES, 1985) underlined the distinction between 'everyday' bullying and racial harassment: 'We believe the essential difference between racist name-calling and other forms of name-calling is that whereas the latter may be related only to the individual characteristics of a child, the former is a reference not only to the child but also by extension to their family and indeed more broadly their ethnic community as a whole.'

Elinor Kelly's research for the Macdonald Inquiry into the Burnage High School in Manchester revealed anti-Celtic harassment as well as abuse and violence directed at young people identifiable by the colour of their skin. Language, culture, religion as well as physical characteristics may provide the hooks for racial harassment, and one will be aware of the upsurge in anti-Muslim sentiments and actions during the Salman Rushdie Affair and the Gulf War. Similarly long-established members of the Irish communities have suffered extremes of harassment as a result of the media treatment of the 'Northern Ireland Question'. However, the crudest and most destructive forms of abuse and violence are directed against people perceived as different by virtue of the colour of their skin.

The effects

Research has been carried out, reports have been written and recommendations have been made over many years but very little has changed for many children in British society. Children may refuse to go to school or play truant. They may develop psychological problems and require counselling. They may under-achieve or fail at their school work. For some even academic success is achieved at the cost of self-esteem, peace of mind and security.

And the experiences of the individual affect the well-being of the rest of the family. Parents watch helplessly while their offspring exhibit symptoms of fear and depression. They may mention the problem. The parents may attempt to encourage or reassure with a variety of traditional homilies. They may suggest intervening only for the child to say that, if they do, the situation will get worse. And when they finally do so, often the child is right. Disillusionment sets in. And since this is an issue that is not generally shared for discussion either with the pupils in a school, for example, and their parents, then the belief grows that there may be something inherently at fault with the victim.

Why do bullying and racial harassment persist? Unfortunately, institutions, because of the way they are organised around rules, procedures and particular priorities, in other words in the way that their members and activities are 'institutionalised', may inspire or provoke individuals or groups to mistreat others perceived as different from themselves and somehow therefore less deserving of respect. Such mistreatment is then itself institutionalised in the acceptance of the tradition of not 'snitching' or telling tales.

Adults in charge may very well respond to attempts at reporting with rejoinders of 'Sticks and stones may break my bones but names will never hurt me', a hoary old myth that is an excuse for indifference. They may well say that 'It is a big bad world out there – the sooner you get used to it the better!' This is the same as saying that schooling is a preparation for accepting the intolerable, a counsel of despair.

This is the unfortunate negative spiral of individual conditioning and impersonal and inflexible procedures that put institutional considerations above those of the individual. This situation is further aggravated in schools by factors such as the increasingly centralised control of narrowly focused curricula and assessments and tests conducted in a context of competitive league tables seemingly as much obsessed with failure as with anything else.

The problem

If the people involved in running schools, residential homes and youth clubs can begin to understand the inherent problems of the institutions in their charge and the likelihood of mistreatment, they can move along the continuum from authoritarianism to democracy by attempting to create a community based on respecting individuals and valuing diversity of all kinds. This will involve openness, participation and accountability at every level.

Those are admirable principles, of course, but hard-pressed teachers and youth workers, perplexed parents and confused pupils will need something more tangible than a mere enunciation of principle or a statement of policy. Far too often, however, teachers and others at the sharp end of the organisation are asked to deal with a massive, long-standing problem without guidance, support, training, resources or indeed the time and space to concentrate on developing the conditions to produce responsible citizens rather than obedient subjects.

One solution

This is where such well devised programmes as the Heartstone Project can help. It is based on an exciting story, *The Heartstone Odyssey*, which spans space and time and weaves a web of magic to transform an otherwise deformed reality. It is a gripping story tracing events, relationships and motives in India under the Raj and modern multi-ethnic post-war Britain where animals and people can talk to each other, and where it is the little ones, the mice, that inspire the effort and co-operation required to change the course of history and transform the world and the people in it. Like all good stories, it turns logic on its head and shows the readers new ways of standing up courageously and with determination for justice and equality. It challenges prejudice and stereotypes with a range of human examples of integrity and courage in a variety of everyday settings.

It lends itself to activities in school such as morning assembly, cross-curricular projects, Personal and Social Education themes and extra-curricular programmes reaching out into the wider community as well. It has now grown into an all-embracing national project with overseas connections covering many schools and LEAs in Britain. And it has the advantage of being adopted in a variety of settings where the number of participants, the time allocated to the project, the methodology and the number of adults involved are tailor-made to local needs. Feedback and information about models of good practice further inform advice, training and the provision of support materials.

The moving spirit behind the project is Sita Kumari, a dancer and an organiser of energy, imagination and distinction, who has from the beginning seen the project's potential for facilitating the growth of individuals and communities to ensure mutual respect and co-operation as well as achievement and the realisation of individual and group potential.

She has successfully piloted the project and the materials aimed at exciting children's curiosity about the world and encouraging their involvement by helping to shape the conditions in which they are schooled or brought together for learning or other purposes. Educators, carers, youth club leaders, parents and children have been involved in the piloting. Support has been forthcoming from bodies involved in Racial Harassment Forums, with community policing groups prominent among them. From the wide range of experience in rural and urban areas throughout the United Kingdom in relation to children and young people of all ages in all kinds of organisations, there is now a fund of knowledge about the best conditions for adopting the project and ensuring a successful lasting outcome.

The benefits

Academics have been involved in evaluating the project. For example, Sheffield University conducted research for the project that showed a marked reduction in what they described as negative incidents of bullying and racial harassment. The researchers noted increased respect and understanding among children and young people. One will recall the Elinor Kelly research (1988) for the Macdonald Inquiry into the killing of Ahmed Iqbal Ullah in the Burnage High School playground showing the experiences of 13- and 15-year-olds in relation to racism – a substantial group subscribing to National Front ideas, an equally large group committed to racial justice but with a profound difference in the terminology and framework for action available to both, with the latter group at a considerable disadvantage in implementing their principles. Such negative conditions will not disappear of themselves. They require commitment and a practical framework in which people can operate to create and preserve a positive ethos. This is what the Heartstone Project does.

The research also showed enhanced literacy and communication skills. That should not be surprising. If one learns in congenial, secure, unthreatening conditions, it is likely that one's energies may be directed at all-round progress instead of having to be used for survival and defending one's space. Children in such situations are more likely to support, help and encourage each other in all aspects of their lives – social, emotional and intellectual. One will recall the experiences of children involved in *Eye of the Storm* – the video of the experiment carried out with white children in a small mid-West town when Martin Luther King was assassinated. The teacher tested the children before, during and after the experiment. Academic progress was marked and sustained as a result of their experiences in tackling attitudinal and institutional racism. And when they came together with their teacher some 20 years later, it was clear that this experience had imprinted itself on their minds. As with the Heartstone Project, when adults demonstrate their belief that children and young people are capable of applying their minds individually and collectively to complex moral and social issues, they respond to the challenge and to the adults' expectations of them.

In a lecture to the National Foundation for Educational Research, Julia Dreyden (1989) spoke about the problems of oppressed groups, just like those who are bullied or racially harassed, who are not allowed to use their reservoirs of energy in realising their individual human potential in secure, reassuring conditions. Doors open for those who are white, male and middle-class. The attractive, gracious and graceful are welcomed and encouraged. The gauche, the awkward, the slow and the clumsy receive messages from individuals and the system that confirm their perceived shortcomings. A combination of negative prejudice, destructive stereotyping and low expectations help to create a pecking order in which bullying and racial harassment flourish. What the Heartstone Project does is to create a secure environment where people are treated with respect and valued equally. In such conditions energy can be used individually and on a corporate basis to regenerate and transform self and community. The change is palpable and those involved can see that their efforts are worthwhile. That experience in turn inspires further effort towards developing even higher standards of self-discipline and mutual respect and co-operation.

Another important result of the project that has been documented has been the experience of being involved in considering equal opportunities issues leading to the development of practical, implementable policies and guidelines. There are clear advantages to be gained by community ownership of policies – the community means not only teachers, social workers and other professionals but children and parents. It is not only the children who are bullied and racially harassed who become disillusioned but their parents as well. In the case of schools, if the policies are regularly proclaimed, and if mutual respect, self-discipline, a sense of the occasion and co-operation are clearly explicit in all the activities of the school – morning assembly, formal lessons, extra-curricular activities, morning break and lunch-time, the toilets, the corridors, the playground, arrival and departure on foot or by public transport – and if the teachers present good role models committed to safeguarding the welfare of all their pupils, it is then that institutions start to be transformed into welcoming learning communities integrated into the realities of life around them.

Fitting it in

One envisages devoting about one hour a week to the project in schools, within the existing curriculum, of course, where it also has cross-curricular potential. There is the possibility of using a morning assembly, for example, as a regular means of presenting items by the pupils themselves. Through drama, dance, creative writing, there can be meaningful presentations about issues of importance to children and young people. Because the children and young people are involved in planning, implementing and evaluating the project, there is a shared determination to see the project through to successful completion. There is also the advantage of having a substantial group talking about the project and what they are gaining from it within the institution and to people outside such as their parents and friends. There is no substitute for this kind of word-of-mouth publicity when real satisfaction is spontaneously expressed by sincere young people whose interest is in a shared well-being rather than in elaborate public relations exercises.

Some of the worst experiences for children are those resulting from their regular or systematic isolation or rejection by others, especially peers. These are experiences which children will have picked up their parents and other adults from their early years. They may made to sit in the corner in their play group or sent to their room at home. Adult contact may have been withdrawn, along with a visible temporary loss of love and goodwill, for acts perceived by adults as offensive. Children learn to manipulate relationships in the same way. The victims of rejection or isolation in relation to their peer group are further perplexed when those who appeared to be their friends are in turn pressured to conspire in their rejection.

The Heartstone Project allows young people to share their experiences of such things within a secure framework where mutually acceptable ground rules have been laid. The ground rules exercise itself is important in promoting the idea of respect and consideration: how should we conduct this exercise? How should we arrange it for people to speak in turn? How can we ensure that everybody gets an opportunity to speak? How do we listen to each other? Since matters of this kind are intensely personal, how do we ensure that existing alliances and resentments do not obstruct the effective airing of issues? What about confidentiality so that contributors may talk without fear of mockery and gossip later?

Story Circles

The Heartstone Odyssey book and the linked photographs contained in the Heartstone Pack can be used in Story Circles – the name given to groups participating in the Heartstone Project – to provide a forum for discussion on a whole range of experiences of intolerance of all kinds. The children will set the agenda and the rules once they are given the freedom, encouragement and the setting to do so. They will appreciate the resulting secure environment for the free expression of experiences and feelings by both victims and perpetrators. They will find a route thereby to a working consensus about relationships, mutual respect, co-operation and equal just treatment.

Another valuable outcome of the project will be enhanced relationships with adults who have a range of significant roles in relation to young people – parents, teachers, youth leaders, police, shopkeepers, social workers, bus drivers and many others. There will be an opportunity to work out agreed strategies together when adults too accept responsibilities within an agreed, negotiated, non-authoritarian framework. They will develop and flourish more effectively from example, from practice, rather than precept alone. Children and young people have a lot to teach adults about conditions conducive to good order and co-operation. Very often the adults will act as facilitators and allow the Heartstone discussion to run, intervening only in the early stages when things become heated. Their best contributions will also be as equals when they describe their own feelings of bullying and harassment as young people and even in their present roles at the hands of groups of young people and their peers in the workplace. This is when adults and young people together are arriving at an analysis that places the problem in its historical context as well so that there can be a true understanding of the forces that conspire in oppression and the misuse of power.

Part of the project has to do with overseas contacts and experiences. The international social and environmental programme presents a clear, direct challenge to what have been allowed to develop as unacceptable social and living conditions as well as an intolerable deteriorating environment threatening not just the next generation but the present one. This is an important way of challenging the stereotypical views that young people and adults have been conditioned to develop about people in other parts of the world that we describe as the under-developed or developing world.

The project provides important opportunities to appreciate linguistic and cultural diversity at home and abroad as well as the multi-faith nature of the world in which we live. The former also includes con-sideration of class divisions and the prejudices directed at dialect and accent which are so potent in teaching people to 'know their place' as somehow inferior in relation to academic potential and all-round achievement. Community languages and bi- and multilingualism will be skills that young people will declare as an asset instead of concealing because conditioning has taught people in Britain to accept the inferiority of Asian and African languages and the Caribbean variants of English. The positive consideration of different religious faiths and practices and their places of worship will enable young people to develop the principle of tolerance in its broadest, most vital sense and to bring a critical understanding to outbreaks of anti-Muslim feeling during such events as the Salman Rushdie Affair and the Gulf War as well as to the sporadic desecration of Jewish cemeteries.

Proven positive outcomes

The project brings about a range of important outcomes. There are enhanced life chances for all those involved through the realisation of potential individually and communally. There are demonstrably improved standards of literacy and communication which are fundamental to academic progress, of course. There is increased self-confidence in combating harassment and bullying, and a growth of positive self-esteem, self-image and identity. Who am I? What am I? Why? These are questions that young people will be free to ask and to answer without the distractions of unwarranted challenges to their sense of self-worth. One will understand in this regard the importance that Jocelyn Maxime and her Centre for Advancement attach to *racial* identity for black children growing up in a society such as this. The absence of positive role models and a range of relevant play and learning resources in the early years deprives many young black children of the opportunity to feel accepted as they are along with other members of their communities. The Heartstone Project is one way to fill that gap in the experience of young people.

All these elements are part of the warp and the weft of promoting autonomy and assertiveness as well as the capacity for valuing and respecting others equally, that is not just in theory but in practice and in the detail of day to day living.

The project covers a wide age range – 8 to 18 years – and can be used in schools, residential homes and youth clubs. With junior groups (aged 8 to 12) the Story Circle caters for between 30 and 36 pupils. Similar groups are established with older children although less emphasis is placed here on the Heartstone Odyssey book and more on the images and overseas contacts in conjunction with the exhibition photographs which are captioned. This is an opportunity for the children to relate parts of the story and the scenes depicted in the photographs to their own personal experiences. This is a demonstration of the relevance of schooling which is so important if children are not to become disillusioned with education and its prospects for them.

Young people involved in the project work towards building their own Heartstone Exhibition or wall display, including a charter worked out by the group. Each pack contains a specific charter pack along with VIP quotes from people like Desmond Tutu, for example. He is an attractive, charismatic role model, much in the news, known to the children, worthy of admiration in the struggle for justice in South Africa and especially outstanding in demonstrating tolerance to others after the struggle for freedom has been won. His presence as one of the Charter's VIPs lends weight to the charter created by the children and young people themselves as an effective means of countering racial harassment.

Young people become absorbed in the production of a charter relevant to their own situation and to their aspirations for mutual respect and good relations. Depending on the age group and the skill levels, the charter assumes many forms from the spontaneous and direct to the more considered and sophisticated. Whatever the finished product, however, the significance of the charter lies in the declarations of qualities that young people want to see in themselves and others as a vital contribution to creating congenial conditions for learning and being. The charter may caution against a number of different negative attitudes and postures in the community such as 'Don't judge people by their appearances', 'We don't want bullying or racism', 'We don't like skitting', 'Don't be afraid to show your feelings' and 'Don't be afraid to speak up'. It also includes positive exhortations such as 'Respect other people's religions', 'Treat people the way you would like to be treated', 'Love one another', 'We should respect all people, animals and the earth', 'If you are friends with someone, be good to them', 'Try and be good in the playground', 'Be kind to each other' and 'Play fair'. Children, young people, their parents and their teachers can look at these and see the deeply held feelings that people have about their condition – they can see that these are shared views and feelings, and the sharing puts out the vibrations necessary for changing individuals and the community as a whole.

The Heartstone Story Circle in turn makes the international contacts provided for them through the Project and includes the results in the exhibition. The international aspect is already conveyed in the story of course, which shows the historical connection between Britain and the Asian sub-continent. What young people learn is that there are at least two sides to every story. What they then learn from history can provide a model for dealing with interpersonal problems in their own communities as well as rejecting the distortions and misrepresentations about other peoples promoted by the media and politicians for their own purposes.

It is important to remove – not just bridge – the generation gap between young people and adults in schools and youth clubs, for example, across year groups and so on. The project when used across the years and across schools can serve to establish a solidarity within communities in which at present there is unnecessary division and conflict. What is more is that the project can release those insights that young people have about the problems that they had to face or they saw others facing in similar situations. Sixteen- and seventeen-year-olds are often better mentors than adults in that they are closer to shared experiences and understanding. Younger children often find it easier to seek their advice than to consult teachers who after all are still authority figures whom children and young people perceive as likely to feel aggrieved if their advice is not followed. Young adults can therefore provide an effective conduit of communication and feedback between and children. This is another advantage of the Heartstone Project.

Methodology

How does one use the Heartstone Odyssey story? First of all read it carefully. It is imaginative. It is full of incidents. It draws one into experiences. It actively invites the suspension of disbelief. It gives colour and form to imagination. It pushes back the horizons of possibility. It helps children move from the negative to the positive. Things can happen in this way. Things can change. Children and young people begin to feel that 'I can change the world starting with myself and my immediate environment.' The world can be an exciting place.

How does one then use the story? Does one read it to them? Does one give a preamble? Does one summarise and read passages? Does one get the young people to read? Does one present a group of them reading different parts? All these depend on your practice and your young people. It can be an opportunity for slow readers to play their part, with the teacher or the parent or their peers helping them by careful coaching or rehearsal to present themselves effectively. Nothing succeeds like success.

Or perhaps one takes the story as a jumping off point to deal with the incidents that are important to the children – and this may be the way in the lower years of secondary schools, for example. Ultimately there is no single or 'right' way to use the material. What is provided is a range through which the issues of intolerance leading to bullying can be raised in a safe, comfortable and natural way. Particular relationships, special circumstances, the unique occasion, the never-to-be-missed opportunities offered and the penetrating insights and deep awareness brought to them by children, young people and adults will determine what is best to secure understanding and progress.

Summary

To sum up, the project has been adopted in a variety of settings such as schools, residential homes and youth clubs. It depends for its success on being child/young person-centred with all of them very directly involved and giving their unique thrust and direction to the activities around the project. Secondly, the Heartstone Exhibition grows organically and visibly from Day One by use of the photographs in the pack. It is not a sudden culmination appearing from nowhere as it were but a growing chart of illustration and achievement. Thirdly, the books and the images must be used side by side for the fullest effect. The pictures give another dimension of the Heartstone experience – the story is the opportunity for the imaginative journey, the flight of fantasy, crossing and criss-crossing space and time, walking in other people's moccasins and developing empathy while the pack brings in the reality of people's lives, one balancing and augmenting the nature and quality of the other. Fourthly, overseas contacts are available for everyone involved, and details are automatically forthcoming within ten days of adopting the project. Finally, Mouse HQ is there to give advice and support at any time.

What better way to conclude this chapter than by reference to the experiences of children, parents and teachers at the Major Lester JMI School in Liverpool? The changes in the children were 'truly remarkable'. 'They became ... aware of issues relating to injustice, bullying and racism and they seek to find solutions. The parents who worked with us got so much out of the work that they are going to join an Anti-Racist Network to continue working against racism .... One parent admitted to being racist and feels the Heartstone work at the school has altered her views.' Other staff have noticed the changes in the children. 'The work has empowered them. They appear to have more confidence to air their views and to listen to the views of others.' 'They showed confidence in asking questions of visitors to the school.' 'It has been possible to link up the whole school in the activities inspired by the Heartstone Project.' 'The children organised a Bring and Buy Sale and raised over £200 to help endangered species.'

This is what education is about – transforming the lives of young people and their communities, empowering them and giving them the confidence to bring up issues which are important to them locally and globally, enabling them to protect themselves and others along with their environment and above all to share a vision about the kind of world they want for themselves and others – where all can be equally valued and respected.

Note

The address of the Heartstone Project, Northern Office, is: PO Box 11501, Huntly, Aberdeenshire AB54 4YG.

Chapter 13

Offenders at school: links between school failure and aggressive behaviour

Angela Devlin

Background to survey

My interest in exploring the links between school failure and criminal offending arose from the 13 years I spent working with excluded children and school refusers, as a home tutor and in pupil referral units. A number of them were already in trouble with the police. Many had been excluded for aggressive behaviour – they had bullied their peers and attacked their teachers. Some had been the victims of bullying and this was often a contributory factor in their refusal to attend school. Others had begun as victims, turned into bullies in self defence and ended up as aggressive as their own persecutors.

Methodology

In 1993, with Home Office permission, I embarked on a survey of inmates in six male and six female prisons, ranging from high security establishments to open prisons and young offender institutions. My questionnaire, designed with the help of a very experienced prison education officer, asked more than 40 questions about inmates' educational backgrounds, including questions on bullying and victimisation.

I received 250 replies, 138 from male inmates and 112 from females, which I followed up with indepth personal interviews, each about one hour long and conducted in complete privacy, with the guarantee of anonymity. I always included the sixty-four-thousand dollar question, 'Could anything have been done at school to prevent you being in custody now?'

I interviewed 100 prisoners – 52 men and 48 women. Although only four per cent of the prison population is female, I had decided early on that I was just as interested in the roots of female as of male offending. Apart from gender and length of sentence (I tended to receive replies from those serving longer than average sentences, for simple reasons of continuity in the same establishment), the sample was reasonably representative of the general prison population in terms of age, ethnicity and range of educational achievement.

Higher incidence of bullying and victimisation at secondary school

I compared prisoners' answers on bullying and victimisation with estimated national averages as calculated in the 1994 Sheffield University study of school bullying, the most extensive British study ever undertaken, involving nearly 7,000 pupils in the Sheffield area.

I found it interesting that while the prisoners in my sample were at primary school, their involvement in bullying and victimisation reflected national averages. But at secondary school, they were far more likely than average to have been both bullies and victims.

Of the prisoners in the sample, 13 per cent (11 per cent of men and 17 per cent of women) admitted bullying others at primary school, compared with 12 per cent who said the same in the Sheffield study. But at secondary school the proportion of bullies was 16 per cent (17 per cent of men and 15 per cent of women) – more than two and a half times greater than the number admitting to bullying in the Sheffield study (6 per cent).

As for the victims of bullying, the prisoners were slightly less likely than average to have suffered in this way at primary school. The Sheffield figure was 27 per cent, whereas in my sample it was 23 per cent (20 per cent of women and 26 per cent of men). But when it came to secondary school, inmates were more than twice as likely to have been victims (21 per cent – 18 per cent of women and 23 per cent of men – compared with only 10 per cent nationally). I was of course asking inmates about their whole school lives, while the Sheffield researchers confined their survey to one school term. Even so I felt my figures were depressingly high.

During the interviews I tried to identify the reasons for the increased incidence of bullying at secondary school level. Many prisoners for whom bullying was not a major problem at primary school had begun to experience problems at the vulnerable transition stage, at 11 plus, from a small caring primary school to a large secondary school. The most common complaint at this stage was a depressing lack of individual attention from teachers. More than half (58 per cent) reported frequent absence from secondary school (compared with 24 per cent from primary school). Many of these were habitual truants from secondary school (43 per cent, compared with only 8 per cent from primary school) – some because of bullying. But a statistic that I found even more shocking was that 52 per cent of the men and 47 per cent of the women did not feel that anyone bothered to check on their absences. Many mentioned being lost in large classes and the phrases 'no time to listen' and 'no time to explain' were repeatedly used in written replies and in interviews. So it was perhaps unsurprising that bullying was less likely to be picked up.

Bullying by teachers

Some prisoners felt that bullying was not only tolerated but condoned by teachers. These words from a woman of 21, jailed for grievous bodily harm, were typical of other prisoners' experiences:

> 'I was always a very quiet child and on my own all the time because the others bullied me. It was physical bullying and it was mostly done by other girls, not by the boys. They'd come up and kick me. I never told my mother and she never noticed all the bruises. The teachers didn't care. They bullied you themselves as well. If I wasn't doing something properly one teacher would hit me across the head with a ruler. I also remember her dragging me round by the hair. I don't think that sort of thing goes on any more.'

Sadly, the accounts of dozens of her fellow prisoners show that it does. As well as the widespread use of hectoring language and inconsistent punishment, there were also some shocking examples of family labelling, insensitive attitudes to disabilities like stammering, overt racial prejudice and sometimes outright cruelty. Bullying by teachers often took the form of verbal harassment. Sonia Sharpe, the educational psychologist who worked on the Sheffield University project, told a *Times Educational Supplement*/BBC seminar (20 May 1994) that sarcastic teachers even instigate some of the name-calling that victims suffer. She said, 'I don't think we encountered one school where there isn't one member of staff at least who tends to use bullying as a classroom technique.'

I found, just as I had found in my work with excluded pupils, a considerable overlap between bullies and victims and it frequently emerged during interviews that many of the bullies were 'worms that had turned': they were picked on by others, learned to fight back in self-defence and themselves became bullies. So it seemed unproductive to regard the bullies and the victims as two separate groups: what seemed more important was to identify the circumstances most likely to give rise to bullying behaviour.

Family: predisposition to bullying and victimisation

The pattern had so often been set by prisoners' family situation. An unexpected finding was the very high incidence of fragmented schooling and multiple school attendance: some prisoners had attended up to 13 different schools, including four or five primary schools. Some were from high-risk groups like circus, fairground or travelling families. Others went from refuge to refuge with their mothers trying to escape from violent fathers. Many were the victims of family breakdown, frequently moving from one temporary care placement to another. But some children were in stable families whose work involved frequent moves – many for example were Forces children. Whatever the reason, this constant moving from one school to another had a disastrous effect on their academic progress and even more calamitous social consequences. Strong friendship groups are a valuable buffer against bullying, but these children were always the 'new kids on the block', isolated because they so often arrived after friendship bondings had been formed.

Charley[1], who had worked as a prostitute to fund her drugs habit, was the child of hippy parents who moved from one squat to another.

'I was never in a gang because I was always the new one. Because I was new there was no gang of friends to protect me. And the clothes I wore were different too. The thing was, I was different from the other girls. The bullying was physical and mental. They'd empty my bag into puddles and I remember once my sanitary towels fell out all over the place and I was so embarrassed. I felt belittled and I was totally on my own with my back to the corner. I felt pushed and pushed and pushed and pushed. There was one girl that particularly picked on me. Her name was Jackie and she was one of the in-crowd. She picked a fight with me and by that time I'd had enough, so I just turned on her. I suppose that was a bit of a turning point because I won that fight. I was more in with the gang after that.'

Very little seems to have been done to support children under this sort of stress. Few prisoners (14 per cent of girls and 12 per cent of boys) felt they could confide in a teacher about any problem. There were no strategies to integrate children who arrived in the middle of term, to help them catch up with academic work or to make friends. I have since found excellent distance learning packages being developed to help Travellers' children, and in some areas the education welfare service tries to set up education placements ahead of care placements. Some EWOs (Education Welfare Officers) also arrange buddy or mentor systems to help in the social integration of children arriving at school after all the others. But meeting the needs of such a transient population will never be easy.

Parentally condoned bullying

Prisoners told me their parents often encouraged aggressive retaliation, telling children to stick up for themselves or to strike first to avoid being picked on. One woman drug abuser admitted to bullying at primary school.

'When I first got there I was badly bullied myself. I was dead soft – I used to cry all day for my mother and all the other kids used to nick my biscuits and dinner money. I went home crying to my mother and she said I had to go right back there and fight them. So of course, now I'd got permission from my mum, and the next time a girl nicked my dinner money I went and gave her a bloody nose! And after that I became a real little bully.'

Many bullies came from families where violence was the accepted response to any kind of threat, where children were taught to lash out before others could strike. These were often families where children were physically or sexually abused.

But other prisoners came from stable non-violent homes and had other reasons for feeling inadequate and for venting their frustration, fear and rage on those even weaker than themselves. The most vulnerable to bullying, and therefore to becoming bullies, were those children isolated by some sort of 'difference'.

Special educational needs

The Sheffield study found that children with special educational needs were up to three times more likely to be picked on by bullies. The men in my sample were three times as likely as the average pupil to have problems with literacy and numeracy, and the women were more than twice as likely. About 12 per cent of the men and 5 per cent of the women were obvious dyslexics – I spent seven years teaching dyslexic boys and it was easy to pick up this specific learning disability simply from their writing on the questionnaires. Yet it had never been diagnosed until they reached a prison education department, if then, and they had spent their school-days being teased and bullied by teachers and peers for being 'thick'.

Ricky, 19, was serving the latest of many sentences for robbery and disorderly conduct. He was never given strategies to cope with his dyslexia, was bullied by some of his teachers and was the butt of his peers' derision because he could never read. At the age of 12, in a frenzy of rage and frustration he returned to his secondary school at midnight and smashed up the office to destroy all records of his failure. He was immediately picked up by the police and ever since then has been in and out of young offender institutions.

Gifted children

At the opposite end of the spectrum, some prisoners had plainly been gifted children, which could in itself be regarded as a special educational need. Some had failed to achieve their full potential because of peer pressure. The case histories of two male lifers are particularly interesting because they reveal how frustration led to bullying.

Jim, 39, became a bully at secondary school. Though he was persecuted at home by his father, a violent alcoholic, he found a haven of peace and stability at his small village primary school and a father-figure in one of the teachers. He was a high achiever there. But within a month or two of joining a 1,000-pupil comprehensive he was already becoming frustrated and disaffected by classes of 35 to 40 where discipline was poor and everyone was shouting and fighting. 'I admit I was a bully', he said. 'I wasn't particularly violent or anything by nature. I just used to go for these boys who kept messing around in the class because they made me so frustrated.' It wasn't long before Jim became a regular truant and left school without any qualifications. Years later he took a good degree in mathematics and qualified as an airline pilot. Since being in prison he has written two books and sold the film rights to one of them – all achievements I was able to verify with the prison authorities.

Les was a very short, stocky man, ten years younger than Jim. He was also serving life, for a murder he committed at the age of 15 when he was about to sit nine 'O' levels. He was under a lot of pressure from his parents who had decided he should become a marine biologist and who disapproved of his older girlfriend. One day he just snapped and killed a middle-aged teacher with a golf club. This violent act, which ruined so many lives, was the culmination of years bullying boys whom Les found annoying:

> 'I was trying to get on and I was frustrated. I suppose I was competitive. I suppose I started bullying because I was a small guy and this meant I thought I should pick on kids first, then they'd leave me alone. So I got a bit of a reputation.'

The odd one out

Anyone set apart from their peers by a physical, racial or cultural difference was marked out as a likely victim. Speech impediments, having to wear glasses, being too fat, too thin, too tall or too short, having a 'posh' accent, even having red hair and freckles could make children the target of bullies or bullies themselves.

Any 'unusual' family arrangements could set a child apart from his or her peers: even in the 'liberal' '60s, illegitimacy was still a dreadful handicap. As one woman (another victim of multiple schooling) said:

> 'I got bullied because I didn't have a father. It never takes long for other kids to discover that sort of thing. As soon as I got to a new school and thought I could make a fresh start, something would happen and they'd find out. Like we'd all be told to make a Father's Day card. Teachers ought to be a lot more careful about that sort of thing but they just don't think.'

Underachieving because of peer pressure

Peer pressure to conform is another, more insidious form of bullying and this had led many prisoners to underachieve. A depressing 55 per cent had failed to pass a single public exam – seven times the national average. In the questionnaire I asked whether they had ever held any position of responsibility at school, such as being a prefect or games captain: 26 per cent had been given this kind of post. Of the remaining 74 per cent who had not, only 18 per cent said they would like to have been offered such a position: the rest said they wouldn't want to 'grass up their friends'.

Candida was a heroin addict whose whole philosophy seemed to be based on the 'no-grassing' culture. She was a bright middle-class girl attending a private boarding school until her parents' divorce and her mother's subsequent financial hardship catapulted her at 14 into a large London comprehensive where peer pressure led her to underachieve.

'I had the mickey taken out of me for my accent. I was good at reading but to be one of the gang I just pretended I couldn't do anything. I was ashamed of being able to read! I remember when the teacher asked me to read aloud from a book I stared at it as if I couldn't read it – just to be like the others.'

This longing to conform drew Candida to try drugs. Her addiction led her, in her own words, to live 'like a rat on the streets'. Her baby daughter was born with terrible withdrawal symptoms and shortly before the interview had been taken away for adoption.

Pressure to join the gang

In so many cases people failing in the classroom had sought peer acceptance instead. A very experienced prison education officer told me:

'Young offenders will often boast about their crimes and say they don't care about being in prison. But this is just a face-saving device. They all have a great desire for self-esteem and if they can't get it in legitimate ways they will go instead for negative self-esteem. So when their peers at school said to them, "I dare you to go and smash that window", they would do it, for that very reason.'

Indeed, the male stereotype of being 'one of the lads' led many prisoners to their first run-in with the law. Others, rejected by parents and siblings, treated the gang as a family substitute and would stop at nothing to gain acceptance.

One in ten prisoners had missed a lot of school through illness and when they returned found they had fallen far behind academically and were immediately the targets of the bullies. Some of the most unlikely gang members were people in this group. One boy, back at school after three major hip operations, said he got involved in gang activities 'just to be part of things again'. Needless to say, boys like this were the last to run away and the first to be caught when police came along to break up a gang fight.

Scapegoating

Many prisoners admitted that as a means of self-preservation they had joined gangs of bullies scapegoating the weakest pupils: 'Me mates used to bully people so I just used to join in. It was stuff like taking other kids' dinner money.'

This was the rule of the mob and most inmates expressed shame at getting involved. Alice, a 33-year-old lifer, recalled:

'I did take part in bullying and as an adult now I feel shame at what I did. There was a fat girl in the school who got more pocket-money than the rest of us and she must have spent it on sweets, so we'd take them off her. It wasn't brutal or anything, just niggling.'

It was depressing to trace the pattern of victimisation as it had repeated itself at school, in the workplace, in adult relationships and finally in prison where these people, often child abusers themselves, were immediately targeted as scapegoats, vilified and bullied by other prisoners and prison officers, as they had been all their lives.

One of my most distressing interviews was with Paula, a remand prisoner who finally pleaded guilty to the manslaughter of her baby stepdaughter and was sentenced to five years' imprisonment. At the age of 17 she had become pregnant and married a much older man, returning from the maternity hospital to care single-handed for his three young children as well as her own new baby. When I met her she was still on remand, innocent until proven guilty. But the other prisoners had already decided she was a 'nonce' and she had just been placed on Rule 43[2] and lived for her own safety in the prison hospital wing. You could say Paula was a serial victim:

'I've always been bullied. I was bullied a lot at primary school – I don't know why. The other kids hit me, they thumped me, they kicked me. But I never said anything. When I got to the senior school it was still bad. I told the head mistress but that only made it worse because the bullies said I'd grassed on them and they'd get me for it. It's just the same in here. When I first came here I was in the main block and I stuck it for six months but then I couldn't stand it any more so I applied to be on Rule 43. They said no, twice. I applied to the Board of Visitors and they said no too. But then I said I just couldn't take any more bullying and the governor agreed to me being segregated. Now I'm with a few others. The girls in the hospital wing are OK and I get on well with one of the cleaners. If we were in the main block the others could easily kill us.'

Repeat victimisation

I interviewed four women serving life sentences for murdering their violent partners. Each one had suffered some sort of abuse as children. Each could be regarded as the ultimate 'worms that turned'. As one of them put it: 'If you have been through violence as a child at home you attract violence. At school, because you constantly fear that other children will hit you, of course they do. And this can go on through your life. You are set in the victim mode.' Another woman agreed:

> 'I don't know if it's because of the way my mother beat me, but I'm only attracted to violent men. I have to have the challenge of verbal abuse, but I don't want the physical abuse as well. Unfortunately they usually go together.'

Bullying is very much part of the 'nick culture' where it is known as 'taxing' and can involve a more sinister version of school bullying – the kind of intimidation for drugs, tobacco or sexual favours where extreme physical and sexual violence is inflicted on inmates or even their families outside. Several of the men I spoke to reported being sexually abused in prison. One said, 'It was very frightening and there's no-one to turn to, not a single person, no matter what happens. You are cornered and you daren't say anything. If I'd reported what happened to me I wouldn't be here now.'

Some prisoners said they were on anger management courses and they found these helpful in managing their aggressive behaviour and teaching them how to defuse a potentially dangerous situation. They were learning to walk away from trouble without losing self-respect and the respect of other prisoners. Others were undergoing assertiveness training: this helped victimised prisoners by giving them the confidence to resist intimidation. It also helped bullies who were so often people with a poor self-image which they needed constantly to bolster up through aggression. Many inmates regretted that this sort of training, tailor-made to address their problems, had come so many years too late. Ironically for many, a prison education department was the first time they had ever received any form of individual attention to address their emotional, behavioural and educational problems. Yet sadly it now seems that with the prison population reaching record levels, and with education, training and therapeutic programmes being drastically reduced, offenders will leave prison without any intervention to address their aggressive behaviour, and the sad pattern of bullying and victimisation seems set to continue.

Notes

1 All names used for inmates are pseudonyms.
2 Rule 43 is the prison rule whereby inmates are segregated from others for their own or others' safety.

Chapter 14

Developing a programme to reduce bullying in young offenders' institutions

Delwyn Tattum

Introduction

Bullying takes place in prisons as in many other organisations, such as schools, workplace, residential institutions for young and aged, and so on. In fact, prisons are a good example of the growing concern about the extent, incidence and seriousness of bullying behaviour in society. Sadly, it is a form of cruelty which is widely practised in our prisons and yet it has received little attention from the Prison Service at either national or local levels. Nevertheless, those who work in prisons or are forced to attend them, would agree that bullying is widespread and persistent. It takes place in adult prisons, YOIs, open prisons and top security establishments, and is behaviour engaged in by both males and females.

Bullying ranges from minor incidents to serious acts of assault, abuse and extortion, and can result in cases of self-harm, suicide and murder. The victims for their part suffer the physical, emotional and psychological abuse of their persons as they try to survive in a threatening and hostile environment. Bullying is directed against the most vulnerable members of the prison community, including those who are regarded as being different because of their ethnic origins, social background, sexual inclinations or physical or mental disabilities. But unlike victims in many other institutions, prisoners cannot go home at the end of the day or transfer to another prison – their experience of victimisation is one of 24 long hours.

Just like others in positions of authority, prison officers can be bullies too and any programme which seeks to address the problem must of essence challenge unacceptable attitudes and practices displayed by staff and the institution itself. For bullying not only affects the bullies and bullied. It also affects those other prisoners who may witness it and remain silent about the violence and aggression – as well as the distress of the victim. For you cannot intimidate and oppress one person without making others afraid too. Left unchecked bullying also undermines the authority of officers and corrupts the climate of a wing or prison.

Prisoners have rights. Incarceration does not mean that they give up their entitlement to those basis human rights of justice and freedom from fear. The Prison Service also has a responsibility to create not only a secure establishment but one which provides a safe environment for all prisoners. As one prison governor observed, 'Prisoners are punished by being sent here. They don't come here to be punished'.

Seeking to understand bullying

Bullying is a complex pattern of interpersonal behaviour and if we are to tackle and reduce its incidence we must first begin to understand what it entails. Too simplistic a view can result in the belief that the solutions also are simple. Elsewhere, I (Tattum, 1989) have defined bullying as 'the wilful, conscious and persistent desire to hurt another and put that person under stress'. And this definition is in part supported by a recent study (O'Donnell and Edgar, 1996) for the Home Office, who regard it as having the key components 'that one individual establishes a position of dominance over another through intimidation and exploits their relative power over time'.

Bullying is about 'Power', that is, the ability to dominate another person and make him do what you want him to do. It is done knowingly and is planned – it is not accidental, nor is it casual. An important element in most bullying cases is its ongoing persistence, which can escalate in its seriousness and consequence for the victim. Bullies have learned that by being abusive, aggressive and violent they get their own way. Bullying is socially learned in the home, at school, about the community; and prison may be the first occasion when a bully's behaviour has been seriously challenged and alternative ways of socially relating placed before him. For what is learned can be unlearned.

The bully does not have to be present for the victim to feel fear and threat – he may be lying on his bed, eating his meal, listening to his radio, and so on. It is the ever present fear of what might happen next which causes the stress. The effects of stress can be debilitating and far-reaching in their consequences, and they diminish a person's capacity to think clearly, to concentrate or organise his daily routines. It can make a person explosive in his behaviour, off his food and cause irregular sleep patterns. In the closed community of a prison its consequences can be dire as the victim seeks ways to escape the pressure he is experiencing. Where the choice is between fight or flight, the prisoner may come to believe that the only way out is suicide or self-harm.

Reasons for bullying

Reasons for bullying are:

> Power and Domination
> Greed
> Kicks
> Personal Satisfaction
> Social Status

These reasons demonstrate that a bully has a lot invested in his role and reputation, therefore it will take a considerable effort on the part of officers and other staff to modify, let alone change that behaviour. It will not happen if a prison's approach is haphazard and unstructured, relying on the unco-ordinated actions of individual officers. To succeed, an anti-bullying programme needs to be:

- Planned
- Communicated
- Formalised
- Sustained

Extent of bullying

In a recent report by the Howard League (1995) into violence in penal institutions for teenagers under 18 years, the Commissioners maintained that the nature of prison life breeds bullying.

> The behaviour of prisoners cannot be separated from the widespread cultural acceptance of the use of violence as a means of conflict resolution. 'Taxing' and trading within prisons combines with the aggressive and competitive behaviour that often characterises male adolescence. The reasons for this are complex but it seems ironical that attendance at often state-of-the-art gymnasiums is compulsory in many establishments. It should come as no surprise that bored, angry

teenagers whose only outlet for energy is to 'pump iron' should resort to physical force to solve their personal problems.

Research by Beck (1992) in a young offenders institution involving 250 prisoners about events which had taken place in the last month produced the results shown in Figures 14.1 and 14.2.

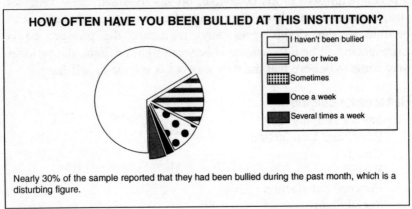

HOW OFTEN HAVE YOU BEEN BULLIED AT THIS INSTITUTION?

I haven't been bullied
Once or twice
Sometimes
Once a week
Several times a week

Nearly 30% of the sample reported that they had been bullied during the past month, which is a disturbing figure.

Figure 14.1

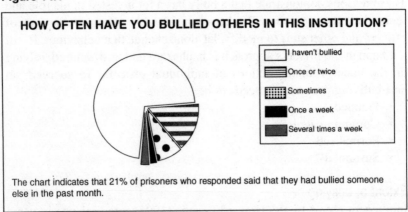

HOW OFTEN HAVE YOU BULLIED OTHERS IN THIS INSTITUTION?

I haven't bullied
Once or twice
Sometimes
Once a week
Several times a week

The chart indicates that 21% of prisoners who responded said that they had bullied someone else in the past month.

Figure 14.2

When asked how often officers tried to stop the bullying, half the prisoners sampled said they 'did not know' and a further 17 per cent reported 'almost never'. This negative perception is confirmed by the 30 per cent who reported they had been bullied, as just over half of them said that they had not told a prison officer about the bullying.

The nature of bullying

Bullying can take various forms, although it is unlikely that any one stands on its own. It is the interrelationship between the forms that makes the behaviour so complex. The six categories listed below demonstrate, in combination, the complex nature of bully–victim interaction.

Categories	Forms
1. **Non-verbal**	The body language and physical messages conveyed by young males can be insulting and intimidating. Gestures can convey both racial and sexual innuendoes.
2. **Verbal**	Verbal bullying can be emotionally bruising. It can include name-calling, taunting, threats, and also racist language and sexual accusations.
3. **Physical**	Physical bullying covers a continuum of severity, ranging from a punch to an assault with a dangerous weapon. It can also include sexual assaults.
4. **Extortion**	This includes forcing prisoners to hand over possessions or bring back valuables, drugs, and tobacco from home visits or when receiving visits. Invariably, baroning and taxing are linked to lending and subsequent repayment with interest.
5. **Exclusion**	Imprisonment separates inmates from close associates. Exclusion on the Wing can further isolate a prisoner's movement and association, hence limiting access to what privileges a prison can offer – *it is a denial of rights*. Segregation under Rule 43 is an act of deprivation – even if it is self-imposed.
6. **Spreading malicious rumours**	The separation of prisoners from their support systems of family and friends makes them very vulnerable to malicious rumours about wives or girl friends – or what may be happening to a son or daughter.

By its nature bullying is destructive. It is harmful to the victims; it is harmful to bullies because its continuation reinforces their existing attitudes towards the use of abuse, aggression and violence; it undermines the authority and standing of officers who can convey the view that it is beyond their care or control; and it subverts the rules of the institution by permitting a criminal sub-culture to grow and create no-go areas in the prison.

Cycle of violence

Bullying behaviour is socially learned and reinforced by inappropriate models at home and in society at large. Living with parents who abuse them teaches children that aggression and violence are appropriate and effective means of dominating others and getting your own way. A bully's parents are very likely to use physically harsh forms of punishment or resort to threatening emotional outbursts. Even if the youngster is not abused personally, he or she may see one parent abuse the other or another member of the family. Aggressive behaviour is transmitted from parent to child, thus perpetuating the cycle.

Sadly, aggressive behaviour can be further reinforced by others in society, who display bullying behaviour in their interpersonal behaviour. It may be viewed on television or video programmes, if, for example, law enforcement agents present inappropriate models when dealing with a suspect. The idea that aggression pays dividends may be further reinforced by teachers who verbally abuse, ridicule or use sarcasm to discipline pupils in front of friends, thus showing them up and belittling them. Equally, if prison officers resort to abusive and aggressive behaviour in their treatment of inmates, they too contribute to a prisoner's hardening attitude that bullying is socially acceptable and personally gratifying.

Research evidence from America, Norway and the United Kingdom indicates that a high proportion (as many as 25 per cent) of young male, school bullies progress through the model to become young offenders with recidivist careers; to violent, adult criminals who are a menace to society; and proceed to engage in domestic violence against wives and children, which presents the next generation of young males with the kind of violent adult models described above and graphically represented in Figure 14.3.

Bullies who end up in prison come from disordered and emotionally inadequate family lives. They achieve little in school, disrupt lessons, play truant and at an early age engage in petty crime and violence. Aggressive children grow up to become violent parents and citizens. To break this cycle of violent behaviour we must intervene whenever and wherever possible.

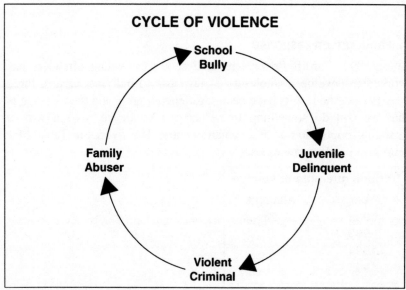

Figure 14.3: Cycle of Violence

The consequences of bullying

In her study of suicides in prisons Liebling (1992) argues that the sources of stress for young inmates are mainly management or environmental in their origins and not psychiatric disorders, and therefore can be countered. She lists factors such as:

Shame
Discomfort of incarceration
Marital and financial matters
Adjustment to prison life
Withdrawal from drugs
Adjustment on entry or transfer
Boredom and isolation
Restrictions on time, facilities and movement

The consequences of these situational factors, coupled with bullying, results in many inmates committing suicide or attempting suicide or committing acts of self-mutilation. In fact, the Howard League's Inquiry (1995) found widespread self-harm throughout the prison population, even in prisons with well-developed anti-bullying policies. A record 61 people killed themselves during 1994, including 11 people under 21 years and 23 aged 25 years or under, of whom 13 were on remand. Nearly 400 people have committed suicide since 1987. The majority who self-harm are young and include two-thirds of all female prisoners. The total number of deliberate self-harm in 1993–94 was 4,187.

A whole-prison response

Since 1993, Cardiff Prison's remand centre for young offenders has worked to develop a whole-prison response to bullying. Over a three year period, the results have been most encouraging and the message is that we can do something to reduce the incidence – even with a changing population as at a remand centre. The figures in Table 14.1 represent positive outcomes.

Serious attempts at suicide	
Year	Attempts
1992	23
1993	6
1994	8
1995	3
Acts of self-harm	
Year	Reduction
1992–93	90%
1993–94	80%
1994–95	80%

Table 14.1: Serious attempts at suicide and acts of self-harm, Cardiff Prison Remand Centre

Many of the approaches we adopted come from my work with schools. In fact, if we can achieve such positive outcomes in the hostile atmosphere of a prison, how much more can be achieved in schools and other organisations.

This section deals specifically with the anti-bullying programme initiated and developed at the young offender remand centre in Cardiff Prison. The programme was conceived in 1992 when a number of officers of all ranks believed that the existing situation was unacceptable. There were too many attempted suicides and cases of self-injury, which were clear indicators of prisoner distress and despair, and bullying was believed to be a major contributory factor. It is generally accepted that bullying has been implicated in the deaths of young offenders in custody, as well as being recognised as a serious problem which needs to be tackled in all prisons.

In 1991, there were 2,963 recorded incidents of attempted suicide or self-injury in prisons. Over 40 per cent of these acts were committed by young people under 21 years. These official figures are probably understatements of the true picture, given the Chief Inspector of Prisons, Judge Stephen Tumim's view that 'too many examples of self-injury are being judged arbitrarily as gestures' (*Annual Report* 1992).

Young people now have a higher offending rate than any other age group, accounting for almost half of all crime resulting in a conviction or formal cautioning. A disturbing trend with this age group is that young criminals are getting younger and more involved in serious and violent criminal activity. This trend has major implications for the Prison Service as there is a consequential increase in the number of 15- and 16-year-olds in YOIs. These youngsters are particularly vulnerable to bullying in all its forms, partly because of their age but also because the majority will be experiencing prison life for the first time.

Crisis-management to prevention

It was acknowledged early in the development of the whole-prison approach to bullying adopted at Cardiff YOI/Remand Centre (see Figure 14.4) that a range of strategies had to be employed if bullying was to be reduced. Bullying was so ingrained in the thinking and behaviour of inmates that officers believed that a thorough and consistent commitment to tackling the problem had to be reiterated from various directions. Initially officers themselves needed to be committed to the policy and its implementation. Moreover, they had to understand the complex nature of bullying and its detrimental effects on all concerned.

Once planned, the programme had to be communicated to all prisoners, and as D Wing was also a remand centre it meant that each new cohort of prisoners had to be familiar with the essentials of the prison's anti-bullying policy and how it operated on the Wing. In some respects, the weekly, even daily reiteration of the programme strengthened officer commitment and inmate awareness.

Crisis-management approach

No matter how diligently officers perform their duties, there will always be crisis cases which have to be dealt with speedily. By its nature, crisis-management is a 'Reactive Response', which waits for a crisis to occur and then initiates action to cope with it. Within the strategies employed are those which deal with individual cases, like the isolation of the victim for his own protection; isolation of the bully with the objective of challenging and even changing his aggressive attitude and behaviour; whilst transfer to the health centre may result from acts of self-harm, which may be appeals for help or protection.

Isolation of the bully was a major element in the prison's anti-bullying programme. The prisoner was segregated from the social life

BULLYING A WHOLE-PRISON RESPONSE		
CRISIS MANAGEMENT	**INTERVENTION STRATEGIES**	**A PREVENTATIVE PROGRAMME**
Isolation of victim (Rule 43)	Helpline	Anti-bullying policy and procedures
14 day anti-bullying programme	Listener Scheme	Induction programme
Transfer to Health Care Centre	Increased time out of cells	Personal Officer Scheme
Counselling – following attempted suicide/self-harm	Education Programme	Diligent supervision
	Recreational programme	Climate of trust
	Meaningful work experience	
	Increased contact with family/friends, e.g. pay phones, more visits	

Figure 14.4

of the Wing and was required to follow a structured programme which aimed at modifying his behaviour and hopefully, his whole attitude towards aggression and violence. The programme could last up to 14 days and had the following aims.

1. The programme aims to focus attention on the bully's anti-social behaviour and tries to modify that behaviour. It is a more desirable alternative to isolating the victim from the bully's behaviour. Moreover, to change one bully's behaviour can bring untold benefits to the victim(s) and other persons on the Wing.
2. As a disciplinary act, the programme removes the bully from his normal location to a holding cell, where he is segregated from the rest of the prisoners and made fully aware of his behaviour and its potential consequences.
3. The programme also has an educative purpose in that it challenges the bully to face up to his anti-social behaviour and presents him with a well-developed programme of training modules to redirect his offending behaviour.

Intervention strategies
Intervention strategies progress the programme into a more *proactive response* to bullying. Unlike the crisis approach, the strategies are more anticipatory and thus seek to prevent problems from becoming crises. Most are social and educative in their objectives and aim to occupy constructively the inmates so that they do not dwell on their situation

and its consequential stress inducing condition.

A *Listener Scheme* operates in many prisons whereby trusted inmates are trained to advise and counsel other inmates. Prisoners are more prepared to talk to fellow prisoners in preference to prison officers, as there is a strong code of secrecy surrounding bullying and its related problems. There is also fear of reprisal if a prisoner grasses on 'so-called' mates. The Listener Scheme is a good example of prisoner helping prisoner.

The *Helpline* is the official Wing post-box into which inmates can also post notes to a trusted officer to tell him about bullying cases, giving brief details about the nature of the bullying, where and when it takes place and who is involved. Prisoners are assured that they will not be identified and that staff will act on the information. Once again, this is an example of prisoners actively doing something to improve life on the Wing. During the Induction Programme they are assured that this is not grassing but self-preservation.

The Helpline is a way of overcoming the highly personal, face-to-face act of informing which many find inhibiting. The Wing receives as many as ten letters each week and very few have been found to be hoax letters or ones with malicious intent. Most importantly, every accusation is investigated before disciplinary action is taken against a prisoner.

A preventative programme

At this stage of the prison's response to bullying the aim is to create a humane and trusting climate on the Wing. Preventative approaches are the most *proactive*, as they aim to predict aspects of prison life where bullying is most likely to occur and introduce constructive strategies to lessen their severity and consequences.

Central to this approach is an unequivocal declaration that bullying will not be tolerated and a set of formal procedures to guide and instruct officers in the handling of bullying cases. There must be consistency in the staff's attitude towards bullying, in the way they investigate if suspicious, and in the way they subsequently handle the case. Staff must be seen to be working together and seen to be in control and running the floor. Ultimately, the regime must be viewed as a positive response aimed at helping prisoners address their offending behaviour – both inside and outside the prison.

The induction programme

This programme (see Figure 14.5) is a central element in the whole-prison approach because it aims to acquaint each new inmate with the routines, expectations and potential dangers of being in prison. For many it will be their first experience of being locked away and for the reoffenders it is an opportunity to familiarise them with the new anti-bullying regime in operation. In fact, the success of subsequent activities to tackle bullying is highly dependent upon the impact the induction sessions have on each new intake.

It is a flexible, rolling programme which can be adopted in any prison system. It runs for five days and aims to integrate new inmates so that

INDUCTION PROGRAMME				
DAY 1	**DAY 2**	**DAY 3**	**DAY 4**	**DAY 5**
INTRODUCTION: COPING WITH CUSTODY	DRUGS AWARENESS	ALCOHOL AWARENESS	BULLYING AWARENESS	HEALTH CARE AWARENESS
MORNING 1. Prison Routine 2. Booklet 3. Canteen Card 4. Role of the Staff 5. Who can help? 6. Personal Officer 7. Allaying fears	1. Types of drugs 2. Effects of drugs 3. Links with offending 4. Health risks 5. Advisory agencies	1. Units of alcohol 2. Long-term health problems 3. Links with offending 4. Health risks 5. Advisory agencies	1. Baroning 2. Taxing 3. Other forms of bullying 4. Helpline 5. Listener Scheme 6. Anti-Bullying Programme 7. Communication	1. Personal Hygiene 2. HIV/AIDS 3. Relationships 4. Help and advice
AFTERNOON Induction Interviews Sentence Planning	Contacting Solicitor/ Probation Officer Personal Counselling	←	ROLE OF: Board of Visitors Chaplain INSTRUCTION ON: 1. Anger Management 2. Face-to-Face Aggression 3. Social and Personal Skills	→

Figure 14.5

they are alert to the dangers of twenty-four hours confinement. In remand centres like Cardiff YOI, the programme has to be able to cater for a frequently changing inmate population and therefore, after Day 1 'Introduction: Coping with Custody', the remaining themes can be dealt with in any sequence. This means that a new prisoner can join with other prisoners on the programme and thus continue to receive guidance on drugs, alcohol, health and hygiene and bullying. Morning and afternoon sessions serve different functions and each is self-contained within the rolling programme.

The four awareness raising themes are interrelated and in many respects bullying is the linking issue as it is the behaviour used to control the supply of and access to the other associated problem areas. Baroning and taxing apply to bullying by extortion and terrorise inmates into handing over drugs and cigarettes. They bring these and other items from home leave and visits, and also to provide favours for the more dominant members of the inmate community.

In some respects, the afternoon sessions follow official guidelines on induction interviewing, counselling and sentence planning. They thus provide officers with opportunities to learn more about the incoming youngsters, take the first step in establishing a trusting relationship, and advise them about contact with their solicitor, court appearances and sentencing. It is a time when contact is made with other members of the prison service who can help and advise – both professional and lay persons.

At every stage, inmates are challenged to examine their own behaviour and present situation and to consider their part in the events which resulted in their arrest, confinement and trial. It is explained that uncontrolled anger and violence are destructive and do not resolve interpersonal problems. Courses on anger management, the control of face-to-face aggression and the development of social skills aim to resolve conflict and are part of the person-changing approaches of this preventative programme.

Upon arriving at prison, many inmates are disorientated, anxious and frightened – they are entering an alien and threatening environment about which they will have heard worrying stories. The purpose of the introductory day is to allay many of their worries and enter them into the daily routine of the Wing.

During their induction week, prisoners are housed on the induction landing to keep them away from the more established and predatory prisoners. Juveniles (15- to 16-year-olds) are helped to come to terms with the experience by being placed with an associate or older prisoner who can be trusted to give positive advice and support.

The Personal Officer Scheme

The Personal Officer Scheme is part of the changing role of prison officers and the whole-prison approach to bullying developed at Cardiff regards this more expansive role as an integral element of its preventative programme. Officers have a more social, educative and supportive role in their interaction with prisoners and work to influence their perception of self and other people. None of this means that officers' custodial and disciplinary functions have diminished; rather the reverse is the case, as officer–prisoner relationships build up trust, reduce anxieties and, most importantly, encourage prisoners to talk about their problems rather than bottle them up. Being trained to read non-verbal signals can alert an officer to deeper, unspoken problems. And whilst casual chats during association or general movement about the Wing are important because they are natural and spontaneous, there is a danger that ad hoc contacts will not be long enough or sufficiently in-depth for problems to surface. Informal meetings are beneficial but no substitute for a formal interview and structured counselling, which are necessary to redirect prisoners' attitudes and values into more constructive channels. For how a person thinks about himself and his relationships with others, influences the way he behaves.

If bullying is to be significantly reduced then the code of secrecy and culture of not grassing, which are endemic amongst young male offenders, must be countered. There is no better way of achieving this than gaining the trust of inmates. In the interpersonal atmosphere of a prison, an early contact with an allocated personal officer provides new inmates with a familiar face, a person to whom they can turn with concerns and anxieties, no matter how small. An improved rapport between officers and inmates produces more relaxed and open interpersonal contacts. It is essential that staff and inmates work together to reduce bullying.

Conclusion

In the case of bullying, there is a pressing need to intervene in the thinking and aggressive behaviour of children and young people and this cannot be started too early. We must present a parenting course so that the next generation of parents understand that the child is father to the man and that inappropriate child-rearing practice will lead to more criminal behaviour. The prison authority is aware too that early intervention means that persons with responsibility for addressing the offending behaviour of young people must act where and whenever they can to prevent violent children from becoming violent adults and a menace to society.

References

Acland, A.F. (1990) *A Sudden Outbreak of Common Sense: Managing Conflict Through Meditation.* London: Hutchinson Business Books.

Ahmad, Y. and Smith, P.K. (1994) 'Bullying in schools and the issue of sex differences', in Archer, J. (ed.) *Male Violence.* London: Routledge.

Arora, C.M.J. and Thompson, D.A. (1978) *Life in Schools* booklet in 'Defining Bullying for a Secondary School', Educational and Child Psychology, **4**, 3 and 4.

Askew, S. (1989) 'Aggressive behaviour in boys: to what extent is it institutionalised,' in Tattum, D.P. and Lane, D. (eds) *Bullying in Schools.* Stoke-on-Trent: Trentham.

Atkin, I., Bastiani, J. and Goode, J. (1988) *Listening to Parents: An approach to the Improvement of Home-School Relations.* Beckham: Crook Helm.

Axline, V. (1989) *Play Therapy.* Edinburgh, London, Melbourne and New York: Churchill Livingstone.

Balding, J. *et al.* (1996) *Bully off: Young People That Fear Going To School.* Exeter: Schools Health Education Unit.

Bandura, A. (1977) *Social Learning Theory.* New Jersey: Prentice Hall.

Baron, S.A. (1994) *Workplace Violence,* Crisis Solutions International 12.

Baron-Cohen, S. (1989) 'Are autistic children "behaviourists"? An explanation of their mental, physical and appearance reality distinctions', *Journal of Autism and Development Disorders,* 19.

Baumrind, D. (1971) 'Current patterns of parental authority', *Developmental Psychology,* Monograph 4.

Beck, G. (1992) Bullying among incarcerated young offenders (unpublished manuscript).

Besag, V. (1989) *Bullies and Victims in Schools.* London: Open University Press.

Bjorkqvist, K., Lagerspetz, K.M.J. and Kaukiainen, A. (1992) 'Do girls manipulate and boys fight? Developmental trends in regard to direct and indirect aggression', *Aggressive Behaviour,* **18**.

Blatchford, P. (1993) 'Bullying in the playground', in Tattum, D.P. (ed.) *Understanding and Managing Bullying.* Oxford: Heinemann.

Blatchford, P. and Sumpner, C. (1996) What do we know about breaktime? Report on a national survey of breaktime and lunchtime in primary and secondary schools. Paper presented to the British Educational Research Annual Conference, 12–15 September.

Bliss, T., Robinson, G. and Maines, B. (1995) *Coming Round to Circle Time.* Bristol: Lame Duck Publishing.

Block, J.H., Block, J. and Morrison, A. (1981) 'Parental agreement – disagreement on child-personality correlates in children', *Child Development*, **52**.

Bond, T. (1986) *Games for Social and Life Skills.* London: Hutchinson Education.

Boulton, M.J. (1993a) 'Proximate causes of aggressive fighting in middle school children', *Educational Studies*, **19**.

Boulton, M.J. (1993b) 'Aggressive fighting in British middle school children', *British Journal of Educational Psychology*, **63**.

Boulton, M.J. (1993c) 'A comparison of adults' and children's abilities to distinguish between aggressive and playful fighting in middle school pupils: implications for playground supervision and behaviour management', *Educational Studies*, **19**.

Boulton, M.J. (1996) 'Lunchtime supervisors' attitudes towards fighting and ability to differentiate between playful and aggressive fighting: an intervention study,' *British Journal of Educational Psychology*, **16**.

Boulton, M.J. and Flemington, I. (1996) 'The effects of a short video intervention on secondary school pupils' involvement in, definitions of and attitudes towards bullying', *School Psychology International*, **17**.

Bowlby, J. (1973) *Attachment and Loss: Separation, Anxiety and Anger.* New York: Basic Books.

Bowlby, J. (1988) *A Secure Base.* London: Routledge.

Brammer, L., Abrego, P. and Shostrom, E. (1993) *Therapeutic Counselling and Psychotherapy* (Sixth edition). New Jersey: Prentice Hall.

Brandes, D. (1984) *Gamester's Handbook 2.* London: Hutchinson Education.

Brandes, D. and Phillips, H. (1979) *Gamester's Handbook.* London: Hutchinson Education.

Burden, R. (1981) 'Systems theory and its relevance in schools', in Gillham, B. (ed.) *Problem Behaviour in the Secondary School.* London: Croom Helm.

Burns, R.B. (1982) *Self-Concept Development and Education.* London: Holt, Reinhart and Winston.

Burns, R.B. (1986) *Child Development. A Text for the Caring Professions.* Croom Helm.

Campion M.J. (1993) *The Good Parent Guide.* Shaftsbury: Element.

Canfield, J. and Wells, H. (1976) *100 Ways to Enhance Self-Concept in the Classroom.* Boston, Mass.: Allyn and Bacon.

Charlton, T. (1988) 'Using counselling skills to enhance children's personal, social and academic functioning', in Lang, P. (ed.) *Thinking ... about Personal and Social Education in the Primary School.* Oxford: Basil Blackwell.

Chazan, M., Lang, A. and Harper, G. (1987) *Teaching five to eight years olds.* Oxford: Blackwell.

Child Line (1996) *Why Me? Children talking to Childline about bullying.* London: Child Line.

Commission for Racial Equality (1988) *Learning in Terror.* London: CRE.

Conger, R.D., Conger, K.J., Elder, G.H., Lorenze, F., Simons, R. and Whitbeck, L. (1992) 'A family process model of economic hardship and adjustment of early adolescent boys', *Child Development*, **63**.

Cowie, H. and Sharp, S. (1992) 'Students themselves tackle the problem of bullying', *Pastoral Care*, **10**, 4, December.

Cowie, H. and Sharp, S. (1994) 'Tackling bullying through the curriculum', Smith, P.K. and Sharp, S. (eds) *School Bullying: Insights and Perspectives.* London: Routledge.

Cox, M.J. *et al.* (1989) 'Marriage, adjustment and parenting', *Child Development*, **60**.

Davies, B. (1982) *Life in Classroom and Playground: The Accounts of Primary School Children.* London: Routledge and Kegan Paul.

Dearing, R. (1994) *The National Curriculum and its Assessment.* London: SCAA.

Department for Education (1989) *Discipline in Schools: Report of the Committee of Inquiry* (The Elton Report). London: HMSO.

Department for Education (1994a) *Bullying: Don't Suffer in Silence. An anti-bullying pack for schools.* London: HMSO.

Department for Education (1994b) *Code of Practice on the identification and Assessment of Special Educational Needs.* London: DfE.

Department of Education and Science (1984) Racial Bullying in Schools. Secretary of State's speech to the Reading Chamber of Commerce, 21 March.

Department of Education and Science (1985) *Education for All* (The Swann Report). London: HMSO.

Devlin, A. (1995) *Criminal Classes: Offenders at School.* Winchester: Waterside Press.

Dooley, D. and Catalano, J.C. (1988) 'Recent research on the psychological effects of unemployment', *Journal of Social Issues*, **44**.

Downey, G. and Coyne, J.C. (1990) 'Children of depressed parents: an integrative review', *Psychological Bulletin*, **108**.

Dreyden, J. (1989) *Multiculturalism and the Structure of Knowledge: A Discussion of Standardised Tests.* Slough: NFER Nelson.

Dunn, J. (1994) 'Changing minds and changing relationships', in Lewis, C. and Mitchell, P. (eds) *Children's Early Understanding of Mind: Origins and Development.* Howe: Erlbaum.

Eisenberg, N. and Mussen, P.H. (1989) *The Roots of Pro-social Behaviour in Children.* Cambridge: Cambridge University Press.

Elliott, M. (ed.) (1991) *Bullying: A Practical Guide to Coping for Schools.* Harlow: Longman.

Etzioni, E. (1995) *New Communitarian Thinking, Persons, Virtues, Institutions and Communities.* University Press of Virginia.

Farrington, D. (1991) 'Childhood aggression and adult violence: early precursors and later life outcomes', in Pepler, D. and Rubins, D. *The Development and Treatment of Childhood Aggression.* Hillsdale, NJ: Erlbaum.

Feshback, N.D. and Feshback, S. (1988) *Learning to Care: Classroom Activities for Social and Effective Development.* Glen View, Ill. Scott Foresman.

Fitzherbert, K. (1991) *The Muppet Club Project – An Alternative Support Service for Children with Emotional and Behavioural Disorders.* Slough: NFER Nelson.

Fitzherbert, K. and Ford, A. (1993) *Running a Short-Term Activity Group – A Handbook for Volunteer Leaders.* Cardiff: National Pyramid Trust.

Fraser, M. (1973) *Children in Conflict.* London: Martin Secker & Warburg Ltd.

Gibby, R.G. Snr and Gibby, R.G. Jnr (1976) 'The effects of stress resulting from academic failure', *The Journal of Clinical Psychology*, **23**.

Gobey, F. (1991) 'A practical approach through drama and workshops', in Smith, P.K. and Thompson, D. (eds) *Practical Approaches to Bullying.* London: David Fulton Publishers.

Goleman, D. (1996) *Emotional Intelligence: Why It Can Matter More Than I.Q.* London: Bloomsbury Publishing.

Gordon, S. (1995) *The Right To Feel Safe.* Adelaide: Mission.

Greenbaum, S. (1989) *Set Straight on Bullies.* Malibu, Calif.: Pepperdine University Press.

Halsey, A.H. (ed.) (1972) *'EPA problems and policies',* in *Educational Priority* Volume 1. London: HMSO.

Hartley, R.L. (1986) 'Imagine you're clever,' *Journal of Child Psychology and Psychiatry*, **27**, 3.

H.M. Prison Service (1993) *Bullying in Prison: A Strategy to Beat it.* London: Home Office.

H.M. Prison Service (1994) *The Personal Officer.* London: Home Office.

Howard League (1995) *Banged up, Beaten up, Cutting up: Report of the Howard League Commission of Inquiry into Violence in Penal Institutions for Teenagers under 18.* London: Howard League.

Jennings, K.R. *et al.* (1991) 'Social networks and mothers' interactions with their pre-school children', *Child Development*, **12**.

Jouriles, E.N. *et al.* (1991) 'Marital adjustment, parental disagreements about child rearing and behaviour problems in boys: increasing the specificity of the marital assessment', *Child Development*, **62**.

Kellerman, J. (1981) *Helping the Fearful Child.* New York: Norton.

Kellmer Pringle, M. (1980) *The Needs of Children.* London: Hutchinson.

Kelly, E. and Cohen, T. (1988) *Racism in Schools – New Research Evidence.* Stoke-on-Trent: Trentham Books.

Kidscape (1993) *Keeping Kids Safe.* London: Kidscape Conference.

Kierran, C. and Woodford, F.P. (eds) (1975) *Behaviour Modification with the Severely Retarded.* London: Holland Publishing.

Kolvin, I. *et al.* (1981) *Help Starts Here: The Maladjusted Child in the Ordinary School.* London: Tavistock Publications.

Kumar, A. (1988) *The Heartstone Odyssey.* Buxton: Allied Mouse Ltd.

La Fontaine, J. (1991) *Bullying: The Child's View. An Analysis of Telephone Calls to Child Line about Bullying.* London: Calouste Gulbenkian Foundation.

Lambourn, S.D. *et al.* (1991) 'Patterns of competence and adjustment among adolescents from authoritative, authoritarian, indulgent and neglectful families', *Child Development.*

Landy, S. and Peters, R. De V. (1992) 'Aggressive behaviour during the pre-school years', in Peters, R. De V. *et al.* (eds) *Aggression and Violence Throughout the Life Span.* New York: Sage.

Lang, P. (1993) 'Counselling in the primary school: an integrated approach', in Bovair, K. and McLaghlin, C. (eds) *Counselling in Schools: A Reader.* London: David Fulton Publishers.

Lewin, K. (1948) *Resolving Social Conflicts.* New York: Harper and Row.

Lewin, K., Lippitt, R. and White, R.K. (1939) 'Patterns of aggressive behaviour in experimentally created social climates', *Journal of Social Psychology,* **10.**

Liebling, A. (1992) *Suicides in Prison.* London: Routledge.

Lytton, J. (1990) 'Child and parent effects in boys' behaviour disorder: a reinterpretation', *Developmental Psychology.*

Maines, B and Robinson, G. (1991) 'Don't beat the bullies', *Educational Psychology in Practice,* **7.**

Manufacturing, Scientific & Finance Union (MFS) (1995) *Bullying at Work: How to Tackle It.* Bishop's Stortford: MSF Health and Safety Office.

McDougall, W. (1908) *Introduction to Social Psychology.* London: Methuen.

McGillicuddy-de Lisi, A.V. (1982) 'Parental beliefs about developmental process', *Human Development,* **25.**

McGuinnes, J. (1989) *A Whole School Approach to Pastoral Care.* London: Kogan Page.

McGuire, J. and Richman, N. (1986) 'The prevalence of behaviour problems in three types of pre-school groups', *Journal of Child Psychology and Psychiatry,* **27.**

Miller, P. and Sperry, L.L. (1987) 'The socialisation of anger and aggression', *Merrill-Palmer Quarterly,* **33.**

Mooney, A., Creeser, R. and Blatchford, P. (1991) 'Children's views on teasing and fighting in junior schools', *Educational Research,* **33.**

Morgan, A. (1995) 'Taking responsibility: working with bullying and teasing in schools', *Schooling and Education, Dulwich Centre Newsletters* 2 and 3.

Mullender, A. and Ward, D. (1991) *Self-Directed Group Work: Users Taking Action for Empowerment.* London: Whiting and Birch.

Murray-Parkes, C. (1971) 'Psycho-social transitions; a field study', *Social Science and Medicine,* **5.**

National Confederation of Parent Teachers Associations (1996) *Echoes of*

Bullying. Cumbria: NCPTA.

Nelson-Jones, R. (1983) *Practical Counselling Skills.* London: Cassell.

Oaklander, V. (1969) *Windows to Our Children.* Real People Press.

O'Donnell, I. and Edgar, K. (1996) *The Extent and Dynamics of Victimisation in Prisons* (Revised Report). Oxford: Centre for Criminological Research, University of Oxford.

Olweus, D. (1978) *Aggression in the Schools: Bullies and Whipping Boys.* Washington D.C.: Hemisphere.

Olweus, D. (1980) Familial and temperamental determinants of aggressive behaviour in adolescent boys: a causal analysis', *Developmental Psychology,* **16**.

Olweus, D. (1991) 'Bully/victim problems among school children: basic facts and effects of a school based intervention program', in Pepler, D. and Rubin, K. (eds) *The Development and Treatment of Childhood Aggression.* Hilldale, N.J.: Earlbaum.

Olweus, D. (1993) *Bullying in Schools: What We Know and What We Can Do.* Oxford: Blackwell.

Olweus, D. (1991) 'Bullying at school: basic facts and effects of a school-based intervention programme', *Journal of Child Psychology and Psychiatry,* **35**, 7.

O'Moore, M. (forthcoming, 1997) 'The Irish national survey into Bullying', *Irish Journal of Psychology* (Special Edition).

Parke, R.D. and Slaby, R.G. (1983) 'The development of aggression', in Maissen, P.H., (ed.) *Handbook of Child Psychology* (Fourth edition) (Volume 4). New York: John Wiley.

Patterson, G.R. (1982) *Coercive Family Process*: Eugene, Oreg. Castilla.

Patterson, G.R. (1986) 'Maternal rejection: determinant or product of deviant clutch behaviour', in Hartup, W. and Rubin, Z. (eds) *Relationships and development.* Hilldale, New York: McGraw Hill.

Pavey, D. (1979) *Art-Based Games.* London: Methuen.

Pawluk, C.J. (1989) 'Social constructions of teasing', *Journal for the Theory of Social Behaviour,* **19**.

Phillips, D. (1989) *How to Give Your Child A Great Self Image.* New York: Random House.

Premack, D. and Woodruff, G. (1978) 'Does the chimpanzee have a theory of mind?', *Behavioural and Brain Sciences,* **4**.

Prutzman, P. (1988) *The Friendly Classroom for a Small Planet.* Philadelphia: New Society Publishers.

Quinn, M. and T. (1987) *What Can A Parent Do? The Veritas Parenting Programme.* Ireland: Family Caring Trust.

Randall, P.E. (1997) *A Community Approach to Bullying.* Stoke-on-Trent: Trentham Books.

Randall, P.E. (1997) *Adult Bullying.* London: Routledge.

Rivers, I. and Smith, P.K. (1994) 'Types of bullying behaviour and their correlates', *Aggressive Behaviour,* **20**.

Robinson, G. and Maines, B. (1994) 'Who manages pupil behaviour? Assertive discipline – a blunt instrument for a fine task', *The Journal for Pastoral Education and Personal & Social Education*, **12**, 3.

Robinson, P. and Stacey, H. (1996) *Let's Mediate: A Curriculum Process for Schools.* Bristol: Lame Duck Publishing.

Robinson, P. with Briggs, M. and Fudge, D. (1993) *Effective Practice in Birmingham: Some Positive Steps to Improve Attendance at Your School.* Birmingham City Council Education Department.

Robson, M. (1994) 'Working with groups on sensitive issues', in Foot, H., Howe, C., Anderson, A., Tomie, A. and Warden, D. (eds) *Group and Interactive Learning.* Southampton, Boston, Mass.: Computational Mechanics Publications.

Rogers, C. (1957) 'The necessary and sufficient conditions of therapeutic personality change', *Journal of Consulting Psychology*, **21**.

Rogers, C. (1965) *Client-Centred Therapy.* London: Constable.

Rogers, C. (1973) 'My philosophy on interpersonal relationships', *Journal of Humanistic Psychology*, **28**, 5, Spring.

Ross, D. M. (1996) *Childhood Bullying and Teasing.* Alexandria, Va.: American Counselling Association.

Rubin, K.H. and Mills, S.L. (1992) 'Parent's thoughts about children's socially adaptive and maladaptive behaviours: stability, change and individual differences', in Sigel, I., Goodnow, J. and McGullicuddy-deLisi, A.W. (eds) *Parental Belief Systems.* Hilldale, Lawrence Erlbaum.

Rubin, Z. (1980) *Children's Friendships.* London: Fontana.

SCAA (1996) *Consultation on values in education and the community.* Middlesex: SCAA.

Schiffer, M. (1976) 'The Synergy of Children's Group Psychology and Child Growth and Development', in *Group Therapy an Overview.*

Sharp, S. and Thompson, D.A. (1994) 'The role of whole school policies in tackling bullying behaviour in schools' in Sharp, S. and Smith, P.K. (eds) *Tackling Bullying in Your School.* London: Routledge.

Sharp, S., Cowie, H. and Smith, P.K. (1994) 'How to respond to bullying behaviour', in Sharp, S. and Smith, P.K. (eds) *Tackling Bullying in Your School.* London: Routledge.

Shaw, K. (1991) 'Setting up peer support groups: one school's INSET response to the "Elton Report"', *Pastoral Care*, **9**, 4.

Siegel, I.E. (1982) 'The relationship between parental distancing strategies and the child's cognitive behaviour', in Lavsa, L.M. and Siegel, I.E., (eds.) *Families as Learning Environments for their Children.* New York: Plenum.

Silcock, K. *et al.* (1997) *Improving Social Competence: Peer Mediation in Birmingham Schools.* Northampton: Nene College.

Silveira, W.R. *et al.* (1988) *Children Need Groups.* Aberdeen University Press.

Smith, M.J. (1986) *Yes, I Can Say No.* New York: Arbor House.

Stacey, H. (1990b) Mediation into schools does go: an outline of the meditation process and how it can be used to promote positive relationships and effective conflict resolutions in schools', *Journal for Pastoral Education and Personal and Social Education*, **14**, **2**.

Stacey, H. (1996) 'Peer mediation skills training for life', *Primary Practice: The Journal of the National Primary Centre*, **3**.

Steerneman, P., Jackson, S., Pelzer, H. and Muris, P. (1996) 'Children with social handicaps: an intervention programme using a theory of mind approach', *Clinical Child Psychology and Psychiatry*, **1**, **2**.

Steinberg, L., Lamborn, S.D., Dornbusch, S.M. and Darling, N. (1992) 'Impact of parenting practices on adolescent achievement: authoritative parenting, school involvement and encouragement to succeed', *Child Development*, **63**.

Stones, R. (1993) *Don't Pick on Me*. London: Piccadilly Press.

Sutton, C. (1992) 'Training parents to manage difficult children: a comparison of methods', *Behavioural Psychotherapy*, **20**.

Tam, H. (1996) 'Education and the communitarian movement', *Pastoral Care in Education*, **14**, 3.

Tattum, D.P. (1986) *Disruptive Pupil Management*. London: David Fulton Publishers.

Tattum, D.P. (1989) 'Violence and aggression in schools', in Tattum, D.P. and Lane, D.A. (eds) *Bullying in Schools*, pp. 7-19. Stoke-on-Trent: Trentham.

Tattum, D.P. (1993) *Understanding and Managing Bullying*. Oxford. Heinemann.

Tattum, D.P. and Herbert, G. (1990) *Bullying: A Positive Response*. Cardiff: University of Wales Institute.

Tattum, D.P. and Herbert, G. (1993) *Countering Bullying – Initiatives by schools and local authorities*. Stoke-on-Trent: Trentham Books.

Tattum, D.P. and Herdman, G. (1990) *Bullying: A Whole Prison Response*. Cardiff: University of Wales Institute.

Tattum, D.P. and Lane, D.A. (1989) *Bullying in Schools*. Stoke-on-Trent: Trentham Books.

Tattum, D.P. and Tattum, E. (1992) *Social Education and Personal Development*. London: David Fulton Publishers.

Tattum, D.P. and Tattum, E. (1994) *Countering Bullying: Raising Awareness and Developing Strategies*. Seminar Series No. 36. Melbourne: Incorporated Association of Registered Teachers of Victoria.

Tattum, D.P. and Tattum, E. (1996) 'Bullying: A Whole-School Response', in McCarthy, P., Sheehan, M. and Wilkie, W. (eds) *Bullying from Backyard to Boardroom*. Alexandria, NSW, Australia.

Tattum, D.P. and Tattum, E. (1997) *Bullying: The Early Years*. Cardiff: University of Wales Institute.

Tattum, D.P. and Tattum, E. (1997) 'A Whole-School Response: From Crisis-Management to Prevention', *Irish Journal of Psychology* (Special edition).

Thacker, J. (1983) *Steps to Success, An Interpersonal Problem Solving Approach for Children*. Slough: NFER Nelson.

Tronick, E.Z. (1989) 'Emotional and emotional communication in infants', *American Psychologist*, **44**.

Troyna, B. and Hatcher, R. (1992) *Racism in Children's Lives*. London: Routledge/National Children's Bureau.

Weiss, B., Dodge, K.A., Bates, J.E. and Pettit, G.S. (1992) 'Some consequences of early harsh discipline: child aggression and maladaptive information processing', *Child Development*, **63**.

Windle, M. (1992) 'A longitudinal study of stress suffering for adolescent problem behaviours', *Developmental Psychology*, **28**.

Wolfendale, S. (1986) 'Involving parents in behaviour management – a whole school approach', *Support for Learning*, 1, 4.

Zarzour, K. (1994) *Battling the Schoolyard Bully*. Toronto: Harper Collins.

Ziegler, S. and Rosenstein-Manner, M. (1991) *Bullying at School in an International Context (No. 196R)*. Toronto: Research Services, Toronto Board of Education

Subject index

Author index